# FLUCTUATIONS AND CYCLES IN SOCIALIST ECONOMIES

# Fluctuations and Cycles in Socialist Economies

*Edited by*
CARLO FRATESCHI
*Department of International Studies*
*University of Padua*

# Avebury

Aldershot · Brookfield USA · Hong Kong · Singapore · Sydney

We gratefully acknowledge the permission for the publication of the papers by G. Ortona and P. Mihályi, which originally appeared in *Economic Notes* and *Soviet Studies*, respectively.

Published by

Avebury

Gower Publishing Company Limited,
Gower House, Croft Road, Aldershot,
Hants. GU11 3HR, England

Gower Publishing Company,
Old Post Road, Brookfield, Vermont 05036
USA

ISBN 0-566-05658-5

# Contents

# Introduction

The study of investment cycles, economic fluctuations or, more generally, economic instability in centrally planned economies (CPE's) has become an important issue of investigation for scholars of comparative economic systems or economics of socialism. In fact, the claim that CPE's are free from cyclical fluctuations and crises, which used to be widely accepted in the literature both in the East and in the West, does not stand the test of recent research work.

In the last twenty-five years a growing number of articles and books dealing explicitly with this argument has appeared [1]. The first 'cluster' of theoretical and empirical analyses of cyclical fluctuations in CPE's can be found around the mid-sixties: at that time, mainly because of the sharp slowdown in growth rates experienced in the majority of East European economies in the first half of the decade, several economists, both in the East and the West, addressed the question of growth instability in Soviet-type economies.

In the following years, also because of the greater stability displayed by these economies from 1965 to 1975 (as compared with the 1950-1965 period), the problem received much less attention: but the severe recession that hit many socialist countries between the end of the seventies and the beginning of the eighties brought about a strong renewal of interest for the subject of cycles and crises in socialist economies. If, as Robert Gordon wrote with respect to business cycles in capitalist countries, we can speak of a 'cycle in the interest in cycles' (Gordon 1986, p. 2) also in the case of CPE's, the most recent years clearly represent a peak [2].

This book contains the papers prepared for the conference 'Fluctuations and Cycles in Socialist Economies', held on March 13-14, 1987 at the Department of International Studies of the University of Padua. The aim of the conference was to review the most important issues still under discussion among the specialists, to offer the opportunity of exchanging and debating their views to some of the scholars who have been extensively working on this topic, and to improve the empirical and analytical knowledge on the subject of economic instability and cyclical fluctuations in socialist countries. To reach this aim, economists from Eastern Europe, Western Europe and the U.S. contributed papers dealing either with the experience of specific countries or with cross-country comparisons, and also with more general analytical or theoretical aspects.

Aleksander BAJT's paper covers various aspects of the problem of cycles in economic activity in socialist countries. In the first part the author, taking into consideration the main theoretical explanations and empirical estimates of economic instability in socialist countries, argues that investment cycles are not an inherent characteristic of CPE's: according to his opinion, instead, they are essentially technical in their origin, and by improvements in planning methods would become milder and eventually disappear. The second part is devoted to a comparison of the causal mechanisms of investment cycles in Poland and Yugoslavia in the postwar period. By using econometric estimates of the direction of causality based on autoregressive methods, the author comes to the conclusion that while for Poland the investment generation of output cycles was typical of the entire period 1949-80, in the case of Yugoslavia causation from output to investment was positive, implying the operation of an accelerator mechanism. This finding is further elaborated in the third part, with the help of a simple econometric model of the Yugoslav economy: the main results of the analysis are that in Yugoslavia the capacity generated investment cycles of the fifties were transformed, in the sixties and seventies, into business cycles, i.e. demand generated investment cycles.

In his contribution, Carlo FRATESCHI tries first of all to show a certain number of stylised facts that should be taken in to consideration in analysing economic instability in Czechoslovakia. In the case of industrial output, in particular, it emerges not only a clear pulsating pattern of growth but a surprisingly regular five-year cycle, especially from 1966 onwards. A rather regular cycle is also identified in the evolution of the 'degree of plan fulfillment' (both for industrial production and for total investment outlays). By examining more closely the relationship between output and investment, it is concluded that: a) the fluctuations in the growth rates of net industrial output depend in a very significant measure on the growth rates of investment outlays in the preceding year, and that the causation running from investment to output seems to derive more from the 'demand effect' of investment on production than from the 'capacity effect' of new investment goods put into operation. Finally, a clear and definite cyclical movement, which also follows almost strictly a five-year pattern, is shown to exist in the case of an important indicator of the degree of tension in the investment sphere, i.e. the ratio of the value of investment projects started during each year over the value of investment projects completed in the same year.

The experience of the People's Republic of China, from the point of view of economic fluctuations and investment cycles, is dealt with in Gianni SALVINI's paper. Six investment cycles are identified in China's economic development from 1952 to 1982, and it is shown that in the Chinese case overinvestment affected economic cycles especially from the late 1960s onwards, although it did play some role in preceding years: in the first two decades of socialist development, it appears that the major role in determining economic and investment cycles was played by agricultural fluctuations and political shifts. By examining the more recent developments, moreover, the author points out that the economic reforms introduced in various steps during the last decade have not brought about the expected results: the most pressing problems remained the inefficient use of resources, the continued and acute shortages of inputs to industry and the excessive investment demand.

The main issue addressed by Károly Attila SOOS in his paper is the lack of periodical regularity in Eastern European economic fluctuations. By concentrating first of all on the relationship between the acceleration of investment cycles and the deterioration of the foreign trade balance, the author develops the concept of 'nearly convertible national currency', which seems to be applicable to the Hungarian and Yugoslav economies: according to this interpretation, in particular, investment fluctuations tend to be rather irregular if the national currency is not 'nearly convertible', i.e. if the investment and the foreign trade policies are not fully harmonised. In the second part of the paper other very important issues are dealt with, such as the existence of time-lags in the effectiveness of investment policy and the crucial role

ix

played by negative feedback mechanisms in the development of cycles: according to Soós, in particular, the one-year lag between changes in investment policies and variations in investment growth does not depend on the completion of complex investment projects, but reflects instead the slowness of reaction of the production (and import) of individual investment goods to demand.

The main purpose of Peter MIHALYI's paper is a cross country analysis of investment cycles in six East European economies: 32 different macro variables are scrutinised in order to depict the consequences of the investment cycle in the entire economy, with the intention of drawing attention to common behavioural patterns during the cycle but also to significant time and country specific differences among them. While some of the results confirm the findings of earlier research concerning the typical response of cycle-relevant variable (like in the case of construction or machinery imports), for other variables (trade balance, allocation of net material product) little evidence is found of any systematic behaviour. The role of the crop harvest, as one of the most important random factors that may have a major impact on the investment process, is also investigated: with respect to this variable, it is found that in three cases out of four the sudden shortfall of the agricultural crop harvest imposed a major constraint on the economies.

In his contribution, Barry W. ICKES examines the cyclical experiences of six East European countries and the Soviet Union, with the intention of ascertaining whether these economies show a common cyclical experience and of assessing the extent to which the observed phenomena are the result of policy as opposed to common systemic elements. The main stylised facts that emerge from the first part of the analysis are that in each of the countries the cycle in output is correlated with a cycle in investment, that these cycles tend to have low frequencies, and that the cycles in the various East European CPE's tend to coincide. In the second part the author demonstrates that, contrary to what seems to be the case in market economies, the explanation of this common variation in East European performance cannot be found in their trade behaviour, or more specifically in their integration via trade. Finally, the conventional approach to cycles based on the separation of a deterministic trend and a stochastic cyclical component is criticised, and an alternative hypothesis, based on an entirely stochastic model in which output follows a random walk with drifts, is tested and commented.

The aim of Guido ORTONA's paper is to explain three main characteristic of post-war economic experience in the Soviet Union: a) the existence of 'waves' of reforms, with quite a long span between one another; b) the fact that, between these waves, the reforms proceed in a stop-and-go way; c) the fact that these waves are usually put to rest quite suddenly. The author develops a theoretical model that analyses the behaviour of a sovereign Soviet-type economy under some hypotheses normally assumed in the theory of the political business cycle with reference to western economies: namely, that the discontent of individuals is a function of disposable income (absolute and relative) and of labour input, and that the government (myopic and with imperfect knowledge) aims at minimising the aggregate discontent. It is shown that in this situation an alternance of political reform and counter-reform may result, even in the absence of any exogenous economic strategy by the government.

In Janusz BEKSIAK's view the economic fluctuations and crises of socialist countries are deeply rooted in the character and dynamic of their socio-economic system. Consequently, in his paper he analyses the long-term changes in socialist economies and identifies a sequence of stages and transformations that are generated by the inner contradictions of the system: the most important driving force is, from this point of view, the contradictory impact exercised on the economy by the traditional control system, which at the same time stimulates and hampers economic activity and development. Tensions, contradictions, internal pressures and economic difficulties stimulate reforms of the system: however, because of the permanent conflict which exists between reform activity and the traditional methods of controlling the economy, the reformed system (at least in its managerial version) is also shown to be highly unstable.

The current debate on cycles and fluctuations in socialist economies is both wide-ranging and lively, and the picture that emerges from these papers shares some of these characteristics. The contribution presented at the conference and the following debate touched many empirical, methodological, analytical and theoretical aspects: the main issues presently under discussion (such as the problem of the exogeneity or endogeneity of fluctuations, the identification of lags and causal relationships between relevant variables, the assessment of political and systemic causes and effects of economic cycles and crises) were all raised and discussed at the Padua conference: hopefully the publication of these proceedings will contribute to a better definition and knowledge of these and other related problems and, moreover, will stimulate further research work on this topic.

The conference, organised by the Department of International Studies of the University of Padua, was financed with a grant from the Italian National Research Council (CNR), which also supported partially the publication of the present book: my most sincere thanks, together with those of the contributors and participants in the conference, go to this institution for its substantial support of our research efforts. I would also like to express my thanks to Sheila Marnie and Josef Falinski, whose help in 'perfecting' the english style of some of the papers was essential. Last but not least, a special thank goes to Bruno Dallago for his help in contacting the Publisher, and to the latter for their readiness in accepting this volume for publication.

Carlo Frateschi

## Notes

[1] An already 'classic' review article is Bajt (1971), while more recent works, containing an update of the relevant literature and a re-appraisal of the problem, are Ickes (1986) and Dallago (1987).
[2] In fact, the first International Colloquium on this subject was held in Paris on March, 1986. The paper and proceedings of that conference have been published in Chavance (1987).

## References

Bajt, A. (1971), 'Investment cycles in European socialist countries: A review article', *The Journal of Economic Literature*, no. 9, pp. 53-63.

Chavance, B. (ed.) (1987), *Régulation, cycles et crises dans les économies socialistes*, Editions de l'Ecole des Hautes Etudes en Sciences Sociales, Paris.

Dallago, B. (1987), 'Les interprétations des fluctuations et des cycles dans les économies de type soviétique', in Chavance (1987), pp.17-44.

Gordon, R.J. (ed.) (1986), *The American business cycle*, The University of Chicago Press.

Ickes, B.W., (1986), 'Cyclical Fluctuations in Centrally Planned Economies: a Critique of the Literature', *Soviet Studies*, vol. XXXVIII, n°1, January, pp. 36-52.

# List of contributors

**Aleksander Bajt**, Institute of Economics, Faculty of Law, Ljubljana

**Janusz Beksiak**, Central School of Planning and Statistics, Warsaw

**Carlo Frateschi**, Department of International Studies, University of Padua

**Barry W. Ickes**, Department of Economics, Pennsylvania State University

**Peter Mihályi**, Economic Commission for Europe, United Nations, Geneva

**Guido Ortona**, Department of Economics, University of Turin

**Gianni Salvini**, Department of Economics, University of Pavia

**Károly Attila Soós**, Institute of Economics, Hungarian Academy of Sciences, Budapest

# 1 Transformation of investment cycles into business cycles

ALEKSANDER BAJT

## Introduction

According to the prevailing socioeconomic theory/ideology, economic activity in socialist countries develops smoothly, without oscillations and at high rates of growth. 'Socialist economy is free of crises. It develops without interruptions, along an increasing line, at high rates of growth' asserts an authoritative source (Academy of Sciences SSR, 1958). The post-war experience of European socialist economies does not corroborate this view. Statistical data show that economic activity as measured by national NMP or GMP (material product, net or gross, respectively) and sectoral outputs of, e.g. manufacturing, construction, trade, both domestic and foreign, fluctuate in a similar way to capitalist countries. Fluctuations were extremely violent in the fifties, particularly immediately after the war; in the late seventies and in the early eighties they probably gained new impetus. While between these two extremes fluctuations became in general milder, in one country, namely Yugoslavia, they were extremely violent also during the sixties. The Soviet Union is an exception: while activity does fluctuate, the amplitude of fluctuation is rather small.

In the late sixties several authors acknowledged the existence of fluctuations in the economic activity of socialist countries. Since

1

fluctuations appeared quite regular, they were generally labelled as 'cycles'. It was almost unanimously agreed that they were generated by investment. Typically, cycles in economic activity were found to be preceded by cycles in investment; it was also typical for the amplitude of the latter to be much greater than that of the former. For these reasons they were labelled investment cycles. For an early review of the investment cycle literature see Bajt, 1971, and for a more recent one Dallago, 1980.

According to Keynes, cycles in economic activity in capitalist countries are also (co)generated by investment. However, while in market economies investment generates cycles through its multiplier and accelerator effects, in socialist economies they are produced by the capacity effects of investment. If Domar's growth equation is borrowed to sharpen the difference, in capitalist countries it is the right–hand side, and in socialist countries the left–hand side of the equation that the cycles come from (Domar, 1947). In socialist countries productive capacities are usually utilised at very high levels — full utilisation of capacities is typical. Thus, when capacities are expanded by investment, they immediately lead to higher output. If investment develops in a cyclical way, the corresponding output aggregates also acquire cyclical characteristics.

Investment essentially develops cyclically because of planners' neglect or outright ignorance of growth constraints. Immediately after the war planners were not only eager to achieve economic recovery from war devastation as soon as possible, but to embark on a policy of fast growth unparalleled in any previous period or in any existing capitalist country. 'Investment drives', to use a then fashionable expression, that is forced massive investment, particularly in industry and above all in its heavy industry, was a natural outcome. Since supply of the necessary complementary factors, particularly of management, at the micro and macro level alike, was inadequate, efficiency of investment was low and, because of the numerous bottlenecks which accumulated throughout the economy, gestation periods were long. If planners were entirely ignorant of growth constraints, they could not fail to understand that by expanding investment, it slips out of their hands. In order to regain control, the investment rate has to be lowered. If this curbing of investment is only temporarily, as is very likely, a second investment cycle develops, then a third, etc.,until, through a process of learning by doing, an equilibrium investment rate sustainable in the long run would eventually be reached, reducing oscillations in investment and output to a *quantité negligeable*.

2

Unless investment is financed by foreign capital, its expansion immediately hurts consumption. Low and delayed investment effects result in consumption lagging behind people's aspirations, a rise in social tensions and political unrest. Supply of labour effort shifts toward the left. Not only consumption, but also output may decrease. A cob-web like movement develops. Expansion of investment (corresponding to production in the original formulation of the theorem) is followed by lowered consumption and, possibly, output (corresponding to prices). The subsequent contractions of investment are followed by increased consumption and output. It is from this scenario, portraying particularly well the fifties, especially the first part of the decade, that Olivera (1960) deduced his psychological interpretation of investment cycles and particularly of their downturn phase. More recently W.Schrettl (1983) elaborated, using a modern analytical apparatus, a systematic theory of consumption constraints to the planners' 'myopic' objective of maximising investment, valid for the post-Stalinist period, working both via the effort-productivity effect and via the social and political pressures on planners. The Polish 1981-82 events are also covered by his theory.

One implication of the above stylised interpretation of investment cycles is that they are essentially technical in their origin, and that by improvements in planning methods they would become milder and would eventually disappear from planners' agenda. In contrast, it has recently been claimed that investment cycles are an inherent characteristic of socialist economies. Dallago (1980) contributes this view to Bauer (1978). According to him, 'investment hunger' (Kornai), stimulated by practically free investment funds, necessarily leads to excess demand for investment by enterprises, surpassing even the ambitious investment plans of central planners. As long as the existing economic mechanism remains unchanged, investment cycles are not likely to disappear from socialist economies.

Let me state from the outset that this controversy is a matter of value judgments rather than positive economics. Bauer's (1978) description is much more relevant to Yugoslavia than to Hungary. Other mechanisms can be added. For instance, when applying for investment credits, enterprises systematically underestimate the financial involvements of investment projects. Once investment projects pass all checks, and their execution starts, enterprises queue up with requests for further credits. Or, they suddenly discover that in order to make the initial investment profitable, new complementary equipment is needed. However, all these and similar practices are stimulated by the first steps toward decentralisation. As shown by Yugoslavia, further steps in this direction may lead to further deviations of actual investment from the planned. I do not think it is fair to blame central planning for the deficiencies of decentralisation. With less decentralisation and more rigid plans, deviations would be lower. Bauer (1978) himself gives an account of an essentially anticyclical method of the so called 'approval coefficients', by which the 'investment hunger' of enterprises is kept within the boundaries of the centrally prescribed diet.

A more positive case is provided by the relatively stable Soviet growth, which displays hardly any visible oscillations. On a priori grounds it very likely results from improved planning methods and greater experience of planners. Frateschi (1980) believes that it is exactly the better organised and more experienced planning process which contributes to greater stability of growth in the Soviet Union. Further factual evidence is provided by the diminishing intensity of cycles in socialist countries, including the Soviet Union. Even for the 1950-66 period, comprising only one entire and about the first half of the second post-war investment cycle (highly synchronised between countries, since medium term plans roughly coincide in time), I found a general and quite fast reduction in amplitude from the first to the second cycle (Bajt, 1971). In a more recent paper Frateschi (1980), who extends his analysis to the seventies, shows that instability as measured by coefficients of variation in the corresponding macroaggregates (NMP, industrial output, construction, and investment) decreased from 0.85 in the fifties, to 0.39 in the sixties and even to 0.26 in the seventies. If these trends are extrapolated, with Soviet performance in smoothing cycles properly included in the sample, arguments against progressive mastering of investment cycles, at least within positive economics, could not easily be found. In spite of this, I do not dismiss the *tant pire pour les faits* on a priori grounds.

Latest developments appear to speak against my thesis, at least at face value. In the early (Poland) and late (Yugoslavia and elsewhere) seventies investment expanded again at very high rates. Similarly to what happened (with all the necessary qualifications) during the first post-war investment cycle, the effects were meagre and slow, if there were any at all. Quoting Trzeciakovski and Tabaczynski, Alec Nove (1986) speaks of the disastrous results of an accelerated expansion of Polish imports of western technology between 1971-75. Yugoslavia can be added as an equally good example. During the 1975-79 five year plan she imported foreign, mostly western, technology for no less than 12 billion dollars, almost 25 per cent of her GMP. The development in Hungary seems to have been similar. The years 1974-78 were also characterised by a new investment drive (Roman, 1985; Kornai, 1986).

4

In all of these (and some other) countries investment was mainly financed by foreign capital. Thus high and increasing standards of living could be sustained throughout the investment expansion. The low and delayed investment effects were not noticed either by the policy makers or by the population. Only when repayment of capital started to fall due, they discovered that even by cutting deep into consumption, servicing of foreign debt became impossible. Contrary to the first post-war investment cycles, when pressures on consumption could be felt immediately, in the last one they were postponed by drawing on foreign resources. Let me add that between these two extremes the actual mechanism of investment cycles was a blend of the prompt and the postponed, of temporarily running current account deficits and depressing effects on consumption, actual and/or expected.

Nonetheless, if this last investment cycle proves to increase variability of the respective macroaggregates in socialist countries, this will probably be a temporary deviation from the trend rather than a reversal. Once it is over, in other words, the earlier tendencies of successive smoothing of investment cycles may return. An additional point is that both in its upswing and downturn phases the last investment cycle was decisively influenced by what one may call an unusual situation in the international capital markets. While throughout a large part of the seventies interest rates stayed below their long term equilibrium levels, during quite long periods even negative in real terms, thus stimulating borrowing of foreign resources, in the early eighties when repayments together with interest payments amounted to huge sums, these were inflated by the soaring interest rates and an extremely strong dollar, with current accounts further deteriorating because of the new oil price explosion in the world markets. Since developments in capital and commodity markets were the same for capitalist countries, these during the seventies also generally embarked on large investment programs financed by foreign capital which, with a deteriorating world markets situation, ended in stagnation and depressed outputs and even more depressed consumption. In other words, as a general phenomenon, the last investment boom cannot be regarded as a deficiency specific to socialist economies. In fact, it was the capitalist system which generated it.

Dallago (1980) claims to find support for his thesis that investment cycles are an inherent characteristic of socialist economies in Soós' (1978) statement that after the 1968 economic reform in Hungary 'the investment mechanism remained strongly similar to that before 1968'. Since in my 1971 article I mentioned changes in the institutional setup as one of the possible ways to smooth output growth, and since I be-

5

lieved that 'economic reforms in Eastern Europe are attempts to move' in this direction (Bajt , 1971), he thinks that the fact that reforms have not succeeded in eliminating investment cycles from socialist economies, clearly shows that I was wrong. However, I never thought, and less so said, that reforms which leave the investment mechanism intact, would do the job. As will be shown later, by radically reforming her system Yugoslavia *did* away with investment cycles. In spite of this factual corroboration of my thesis I do not want to use this as an escape. Rather, I prefer to sharpen it. In my view investment cycles could disappear from socialist economies even without far-reaching reforms of the Yugoslav type. If investment cycles are generated by 'the way investment plans are elaborated' and stem from 'relationships between agencies that make plans and take care of their implementation', they can perhaps be overcome by simple organisational and technical improvements. The real problem with this thesis is that nearly all socialist countries are undergoing reforms that change their institutional set-ups. Not only is *rebus sic stantibus* violated in this way, making factual testing of my sharpened thesis impossible. As is shown by Yugoslavia, reforms may even intensify cycles — though not of the investment brand.

## Causal analysis of investment cycles

So far, research on investment cycles has been mainly descriptive — verbal, simple statistical description and graphical presentation has been typical. Quantitative measurement, if there was any, has been limited to coefficients of variation. It should not surprise us if even the very existence of investment cycles, and of cycles in socialist countries in general, has been questioned. For instance, Klotz (1971) suspected that investment cycles as described in my 1971 article were an artifact of moving average techniques, used to smooth over extreme year to year fluctuation, rather than real phenomena. Also, a given average value of the coefficients of variation agrees with any kind of cycles, agricultural year to year oscillations included. Apart from visual evidence provided by graphs, only serial correlation of deviations of an aggregate around its trend identifies both the existence and length of the cycle.

If an idea based on Kendall (1946), which I owe to Klotz, is used and correspondingly logs of a time series $X_t$, whose oscillations are studied, regressed on a linear time trend,

$$\log X_t = a + bT + e_t$$

where $b = \log (1 + r)$, $r$ being a trend rate of growth of $X$ and $e_t$ residuals around trend, the existence of cycles is confirmed if there exists a positive serial correlation in residuals $e_t$, i.e., if the value of the Durbin–Watson statistic is far below 2. If such an autocorrelation exists, then by estimating a first order autoregressive coefficient $C$ in the equation

$$e_t = Ce_{t-1} + u_t$$

the average period of the cycle can be estimated from $P = 360°/\cos C$. In Poland and Yugoslavia, which will be used as examples of socialist economies which have carried out reforms, far-enough and not-far-enough-reaching, industrial production develops in cycles of an average length of respectively 9.85 and 11.02 years, while industrial investment develops in cycles of 7.67 and 12.2 years (Poland 1949-80, Yugoslavia 1947-80).

Our main interest is the mechanism of investment cycles. Since according to my interpretation these are cycles in economic activity generated by the capacity effects of investment, causal analysis may provide a useful insight into the problem. Econometric methods allow detection of cause-effect relationships, their direction and intensity. While quite sophisticated methods are available, drawing largely on the Granger notion of causality (see for example Sims, 1971, Sargent, 1978), in this paper I shall use a much simpler method. In spite of its simplicity it may prove useful, at least as a first approach. My results must thus be regarded as preliminary.

All econometric approaches to causality start from Haavelmo's (1943) argument that economic phenomena-variables are to a large degree determined simultaneously by a set of exogenous variables. Their contemporaneous correlation is therefore endogenous rather than exogenous, as usually assumed in regression analysis. Therefore, if truly exogenous influences between a pair of economic phenomena-variables are to be established, the endogenously determined part of their inter-correlatedness has to be eliminated and only residuals used in causal analysis. In econometric work which relies on autoregression as an explanation of economic phenomena, it is the autoregressive part of their development which is treated as being determined endogenously. In our analysis we shall treat as endogenous the simultaneous correlation between variables. In my view this is more in line with Haavelmo's original objection than the autocorrelation of individual series.

Without going into any detail, this idea can be expressed by a very simple regression model of the following kind:

$$Y_t = X_t; X_{t-1}, X_{t-2}, ..., X_{t-n}; X_{t+1}, X_{t+2}, ..., X_{t+n}$$

Here, the regression coefficient of $X_t$ measures the degree of endogenous interrelatedness, coefficients of $X_{t-1}$, $X_{t-2}$, ..., $X_{t-n}$ measure the degree of causation going from X to Y, and coefficients of $X_{t+1}$, $X_{t+2}$, ..., $X_{t+n}$ the degree of causation from Y to X. If coefficients of $X_{t-1}$, ... are not significantly different from zero, causation is unidirectional from Y to X; if coefficients of $X_{t+1}$, ... are not significantly different from zero, causation is unidirectional from X to Y; if coefficients both of the lagged and leaded variables are significantly positive, causation is bidirectional, going from X to Y and in the same time from Y to X; finally, if no coefficients are significantly different from zero, there is no causal relationship between the corresponding two variables.

Since at the moment only annual data are available, and since particularly regressions for shorter subperiods will retain too few degrees of freedom, in practical application the above model will be split into two parts, each of them measuring causation in one direction only. These two parts are

$$Y_t = X_t; X_{t-1}, X_{t-2}, ..., X_{t-n}$$

and

$$X_t = Y_t; Y_{t-1}, Y_{t-2}, ..., Y_{t-n}$$

To avoid multicollinearity problems, the two sets of lagged variables will be estimated by the Almon type of distributed lags.

Tables 1.1 and 1.2 summarise regression results for Poland (1949-80) and Yugoslavia (1947-80), respectively. All estimates are OLS, with no constraints imposed on Almon distributed lags. These are estimated by use of third degree polynomials. T is a linear time trend. The rationale behind its inclusion is that it also measures a part of interrelatedness that can be treated as endogenously determined. Running of the same regressions for a model without time trend yields somewhat less clear-cut results. Since Almon lags are for the independent variables lagged one period, the three period distributed lag coefficients are for periods t-1, t–2, t-3 and t-4. All data are in the form of indices, with base year $100 = 1949$ for Poland and $100 = 1955$ for Yugoslavia.

# Table 1.1
## Regression relationships between industrial investment (II) and industrial net product (NPI)
## Poland

| Period | Dependent Variable | Lags of the independent variable | | | | | Sum of lagged coeff. | T | Constant | R²/D | DF/t 0.10 0.05 0.01 |
|---|---|---|---|---|---|---|---|---|---|---|---|
| | | 0 | - 1 | - 2 | - 3 | - 4 | | | | | |
| 1949-60 | NPI | - .095 | 0.070 | - .024 | - .067 | - .059 | - .081 | 23.47 | 91.43 | 0.9995 | 2 |
| | | (-2.01) | (2.59) | (-1.77) | (-4.84) | (-1.57) | (1.52) | (10.97) | (7.29) | 3.55 | 2.920 |
| | II | 1.156 | 1.501 | - 3.765 | - 6.380 | - 6.342 | -14.986 | 263.17 | 467.93 | 0.820 | 4.303 |
| | | (0.11) | (0.09) | (-.46) | (-.44) | (-.18) | (-.205) | (0.17) | (0.16) | 2.78 | 9.925 |
| 1949-65 | NPI | 0.222 | - 0.008 | 0.136 | 0.121 | - .052 | 0.196 | 12.53 | - 8.85 | 0.9928 | 7 |
| | | (1.70) | (-.07) | (2.11) | (1.98) | (-.45) | (1.57) | (2.51) | (-.62) | 1.50 | 1.895 |
| | II | 2.237 | 3.015 | -.320 | -2.396 | -3.214 | -2.916 | 25.46 | -25.85 | 0.9852 | 2.365 |
| | | (2.49) | (2.90) | (-.45) | (-3.43) | (-2.59) | (-1.85) | (1.63) | (-1.07) | 2.31 | 3.499 |
| 1949-70 | NPI | 0.330 | 0.084 | 0.096 | 0.106 | 0.112 | 0.398 | 4.28 | -35.25 | 0.9974 | 12 |
| | | (4.05) | (0.83) | (1.71) | (1.73) | (1.45) | (4.64) | (1.78) | (-6.05) | 1.56 | 1.782 |
| | II | 2.980 | 0.736 | -.079 | -1.003 | -2.037 | -2.383 | 2.26 | -1.027 | 0.988 | 2.179 |
| | | (2.62) | (0.66) | (-.11) | (-1.29) | (1.69) | (-1.62) | (0.27) | (-.03) | 1.63 | 3.055 |
| 1955-80 | NPI | 0.202 | -.073 | 0.110 | 0.119 | -.046 | 0.109 | 22.33 | -87.24 | 0.9987 | 17 |
| | | (5.76) | (-1.27) | (4.19) | (3.68) | (-1.46) | (3.65) | (15.13) | (-5.16) | 1.04 | 1.740 |
| | II | 5.994 | -.683 | -3.666 | -2.062 | 4.127 | -2.284 | -77.79 | 250.79 | 0.9875 | 2.110 |
| | | (4.46) | (-.25) | (-1.98) | (-1.126) | (1.71) | (-1.80) | (-4.65) | (1.88) | 1.32 | 2.898 |
| 1960-80 | NPI | 0.164 | -.065 | 0.130 | 0.122 | -.087 | 0.099 | 28.84 | -181.63 | 0.999 | 12 |
| | | (5.52) | (-1.44) | (6.18) | (4.82) | (-3.28) | (4.21) | (13.43) | (-6.08) | 1.88 | 1.782 |
| | II | 6.916 | -1.150 | -4.536 | -2.296 | 5.571 | -2.410 | -117.78 | 670.88 | 0.9834 | 2.179 |
| | | (4.09) | (-.37) | (-2.04) | (-1.10) | (1.86) | (-1.68) | (-2.97) | (1.66) | 1.62 | 3.055 |
| 1965-80 | NPI | 0.169 | -0.500 | 0.128 | 0.123 | -.079 | 0.106 | 26.76 | -143.48 | 0.9978 | 8 |
| | | (4.19) | (-1.12) | (4.36) | (3.74) | (-1.75) | (2.83) | (3.88) | (-1.23) | 1.89 | 1.860 |
| | II | 6.187 | 0.684 | -6.211 | -3.954 | 7.455 | -2.027 | -76.34 | 19.96 | 0.9751 | 2.306 |
| | | (2.50) | (0.16) | (-1.86) | (-1.34) | (1.57) | (-1.05) | (-.66) | (0.01) | 1.76 | 3.355 |
| 1949-80 | NPI | 0.226 | -.076 | 0.103 | 0.119 | -.029 | 0.117 | 18.24 | -34.96 | 0.9982 | 22 |
| | | (5.46) | (-1.10) | (3.25) | (3.05) | (-.76) | (3.23) | (15.28) | (-3.15) | 0.71 | 1.717 |
| | II | 5.380 | 0.046 | -3.688 | -2.360 | 4.030 | -1.972 | -61.81 | 103.88 | 0.9895 | 2.074 |
| | | (4.63) | (0.019) | (-2.16) | (-1.41) | (1.81) | (-1.72) | (-5.96) | (1.64) | 1.13 | 2.819 |

Sources: Data were constructed from Fallenbuchl, 1984. The missing 1979-80 data for investment were compiled from *Ukazatele hospodárskeho vyvoje v zahraniaí 82*, Praha 1982.

# Table 1.2
## Regression relationships between industrial investment (II)
### and industrial net product (NPI)
### Yugoslavia

| Period | Dependent Variable | 0 | -1 | -2 | -3 | -4 | Sum of lagged coeff. | T | Constant | R²/D | DF/t 0.10 0.05 0.01 |
|---|---|---|---|---|---|---|---|---|---|---|---|
| 1947-60 | GPI | 0.237 (3.44) | -0.205 (-2.17) | -.023 (-.33) | -.057 (-.77) | -.305 (-5.54) | -.591 (-5.13) | 3.73 (13.9) | 22.95 (2.17) | 0.9965 3.31 | 4 2.132 |
| | II | 3.706 (4.23) | 0.152 (0.14) | -2.124 (-3.65) | -1.354 (-1.96) | 2.460 (4.12) | -.866 (-.91) | -12.55 (-6.57) | 77.39 (9.91) | 0.8884 3.03 | 2.776 4.604 |
| 1947-65 | GPI | 0.081 (0.54) | 0.055 (0.28) | 0.195 (1.29) | 0.141 (0.97) | -.106 (-.54) | 0.285 (2.50) | 4.72 (12.0) | -30.79 (-4.02) | 0.9812 0.91 | 9 1.833 |
| | II | 0.093 (0.08) | -1.129 (-1.06) | 0.308 (0.47) | 1.333 (2.01) | 1.944 (1.86) | 2.456 (2.00) | -3.41 (-1.53) | 30.94 (2.71) | 0.8722 1.81 | 2.262 3.250 |
| 1947-70 | GPI | 0.034 (0.33) | 0.041 (0.37) | 0.233 (3.04) | 0.151 (2.10) | -0.206 (-2.19) | 0.220 (2.41) | 4.78 (15.58) | -24.38 (-9.42) | 0.9915 1.27 | 14 1.761 |
| | II | 1.449 (1.69) | -.977 (-.95) | 0.745 (1.75) | 0.984 (1.85) | -.259 (-.44) | 0.493 (0.66) | -5.64 (-2.68) | 51.45 (6.37) | 0.9370 1.37 | 2.145 2.977 |
| 1955-80 | GPI | 0.263 (2.72) | -0.650 (-.53) | 0.122 (1.78) | 0.177 (2.51) | 0.100 (1.05) | 0.335 (3.50) | 3.59 (5.13) | -30.71 -4.19 | 0.9929 0.73 | 17 1.740 |
| | II | 1.002 (1.15) | -.540 (-.50) | 0.332 (0.57) | 0.682 (1.08) | 0.509 (0.58) | 0.983 (0.94) | -5.47 (-1.64) | 55.23 (1.58) | 0.9625 0.94 | 2.110 2.898 |
| 1960-80 | GPI | 0.211 (1.89) | -.055 (-.41) | 0.150 (1.95) | 0.180 (2.34) | .037 (0.32) | 0.312 (2.89) | 4.61 (4.19) | -45.78 (-3.28) | 0.9892 0.63 | 12 1.782 |
| | II | 1.125 (1.14) | -.652 (-.52) | 0.299 (0.45) | 0.771 (1.07) | 0.765 (0.74) | 1.182 (0.94) | -8.40 (-1.52) | 90.41 (1.37) | 0.9441 1.01 | 2.179 3.055 |
| 1965-80 | GPI | 0.119 (3.23) | -.130 (3.21) | 0.101 (4.99) | 0.164 (7.20) | 0.057 (1.95) | 0.193 (6.37) | 8.70 (17.51) | -117.82 (-14.82) | 0.9991 2.77 | 7 1.895 |
| | II | -1.402 (-.90) | -1.085 (-.81) | -.443 (-.55) | 0.800 (1.02) | 2.640 (2.07) | 1.920 (1.36) | 21.18 (1.60) | -354.92 (-1.83) | 0.9426 1.81 | 2.365 3.499 |
| 1947-80 | GPI | 0.245 (2.97) | -.062 (-.57) | 0.134 (2.20) | 0.173 (2.78) | 0.055 (0.67) | .300 (3.76) | 4.12 (14.04) | -36.47 (-14.10) | 0.9953 0.66 | 2.064 2.797 |
| | II | 0.978 (1.35) | -.501 (-.55) | 0.282 (0.59) | 0.635 (1.23) | 0.557 (0.84) | 0.973 (1.28) | -5.09 (-3.88) | 50.79 (5.29) | 0.9737 0.92 | 24 1.711 |

Sources: *Statisticki godisnjak Jugoslavije*, SZS, various issues; *Jugoslavia 1945-1965*, SZS, Belgrad 1965.

In tables $R^2$ stands for the coefficient of determination corrected for the degrees of freedom, D is the Durbin-Watson statistic for serial correlation of residuals, DF are degrees of freedom. The last column gives information on the degrees of freedom of the individual equations, with t-values listed for 0.1, 0.05 and 0.01 level of significance.

In interpreting the regression results presented in Tables 1.1 and 1.2 we shall omit technicalities. Let me only observe that a four period Almon distributed lag structure appears justified by the generally most strong causation from II to PI in the t-2 and t-3 periods; the main exception being 1947(49)-60, where degrees of freedom are prohibitively low. More importantly, longer distributed lag structures might yield less reliable results. It is difficult to believe that causal relationships were detectable by regression analysis for lags longer than four years.

Since the method applied is only experimental, our conclusions are in fact just hypotheses that require further testing. The most relevant seem to be the following.

1. Both in Poland and Yugoslavia causation is mainly unidirectional, flowing from investment to output. Causation in the opposite direction is much weaker and, in general, statistically insignificant at the low level of 0.1. The only exceptions are the 1949-80 period in the case of Poland and the 1947-65 period in the case of Yugoslavia (in both cases significant only at the 0.1 level). From this we conclude that cycles in industrial output are predominantly investment generated.

2. Both in Poland and Yugoslavia, in the first subperiod expansion of investment leads to contraction of output. The highest negative effect appears to materialise after 3 to 4 years in Poland and after 4 years in Yugoslavia. In the case of Poland even the contemporaneous correlation between investment and output is negative. Unfortunately, while in Yugoslavia the unidirectional causation from investment to output is significant at the high 0.01 level, for Poland it is not significant even at the 0.1 level. The much more significant negative causation in Yugoslavia is probably due to the post-Cominform depression, which followed the massive investments after 1947.

In view of these results, the first subperiod appears to be a clear case of planners' disregard of development constraints. Since lower output very probably implies lower consumption as well, this makes the Olivera (1960) type of psychological explanation of the post-war investment cycles an acceptable although not really confirmed hypothesis. Let us note, however, that positive coefficients in no way contradict either the thesis of planners' disregard of growth constraints or the

Olivera type of psychological interpretation of downswings in investment.

3. The negative effect of investment on output is more than overcome (Yugoslavia) and overcome (Poland) in the 1947(9)-65 period. In a still longer subperiod that stretches up to 1970, this effect is much reinforced in Poland and somewhat weakened in Yugoslavia. From this it is possible to conclude that the main changes leading to more normal investment-output relationships occurred in Yugoslavia between 1960 and 1965, when in implementing the 1958 Party program the competences of enterprises in income distribution and allocation were substantially enlarged, while in Poland this was mainly done during 1965-70. For Yugoslavia this is confirmed by the somewhat worsened results between 1960-80 and 1965-80 periods and for Poland by the substantially worsened results after 1970.

Results for 1955-80 suggest that in Yugoslavia factors of improvement were already strong in 1955-60 (consumer oriented policies, complete retreat from forced collectivisation that brought agricultural production to a qualitatively higher level, reorientation of foreign trade toward the West together with renewed access to capital markets). In the case of Poland improvements also occurred already during 1955-60, but they were weak, as in the 1960-65 period.

This allows us to hypothesise that planners successfully passed their elementary school exams already during the first decade of planned growth. It would be difficult to believe that elementary school represented the peak of their capabilities.

The somewhat weaker impact of investment on output after 1965 in Yugoslavia and the much weaker impact after 1970 in Poland do not seem to contradict this conclusion. Investors were largely fooled by the easy availability of foreign capital that made them once more believe that there are no constraints to socialist growth. The much worsened Polish results are explained by the fact that the downturn of the last cycle occurred already in the late seventies.

4. In the above conclusions it is tacitly assumed that investment cycles generation happens because of the capacity effect. It need not be so. However, there are two indications that investment generation of cycles does occur due to the capacity effect.

The first is the negative relationship between investment and output in the first subperiod. If cycles in output were generated by the demand effect of investment, the regression coefficients could not have negative signs. The multiplier effects are greatest in the first periods after expansion of demand. Since during the first subperiod the regression coefficients are negative for both Poland and Yugoslavia, we infer that

12

in both countries investment generation of cycles is due to the capacity effect.

The second is the systematical, i.e. for all subperiods, existence of negative coefficients in regressions of investment on output. The interpretation of this result is not obvious. It could be that investment decisions are to a certain degree independent of market signals as expressed by changes in output. More probably, the negative regression coefficients are an expression of a countercyclical behaviour of planners. Realising that output has decreased, or decelerated, they expand investment, or accelerate its growth, in order to smooth output cycles.

However, this behaviour is limited to Poland. Only for Poland do we have indications that investment generation of output cycles was typical of the entire period 1949-80. In the case of Yugoslavia causation from output to investment is positive. This implies the operation of an accelerator. If so, investment generates output cycles in Yugoslavia via its demand effects.

Although causation running from output to investment, both the negative and the positive, is in general statistically insignificant even at the 0.1 level, the systematically negative coefficients in the case of Poland and the equally positive coefficients in the case of Yugoslavia point to a very different mechanism of instability generation. This result, if confirmed by further research, is extremely relevant for understanding economic cycles in socialist countries and particularly in Yugoslavia, with which we will concern ourselves next.

**Submerging of investment cycles by business cycles in Yugoslavia**

My arguments that investment cycles will eventually disappear from socialist economies have probably not convinced everybody. Fortunately, Yugoslavia has provided us with an example of an efficient way of mastering investment cycles. She did this not by perfecting her planning system but, among other things, by demolishing it. From being capacity generated, cycles in Yugoslavia became demand generated.

This happened with the decentralisation of economic decision making, the granting of greater independence to enterprises and the dethroning of the central planning system. The process started with the introduction of self-management in 1950, continued with the dismantling of branch directorates in 1951 and the abolition physical planning in 1952. The softening of economic policy toward private farmers,

13

which resulted in the expansion of agricultural production, and the shifting of priorities toward consumer goods (1956), did away with shortage phenomena. Thus the economy became a market one, at least at the macro level. On the micro level marketisation was limited to goods markets; even here state intervention in the price setting process has been retained up to now. Capital markets have never been allowed; labour and Dinar have been systematically overvalued and capital undervalued. As I showed at the Balatonfüred conference, almost 20 years ago (Bajt, 1969), the most probable turning point in the shift from investment cycles to business cycles was 1960, although some elements of demand determination of the course of the economy could already be detected during two short cycles in the late fifties (see Bajt, 1972).

In his book on cycles in Yugoslavia, B. Horvat does not distinguish between investment and business cycles. He treats them indiscriminately as 'economic' cycles (Horvat, 1969). While he disagrees with Cobeljic's and Stojanovic's interpretation of investment cycles (Cobeljic and Stojanovic, 1969), in discussing my interpretation he explicitly negates the business interpretation of the Yugoslav cycles. In his view, no business cycles theory is imaginable without the operation of an accelerator. However, he goes on to claim that in an economy based on labour, such as Yugoslavia, this is not possible. Not demand but capital accumulation induces expansion of consumption (see discussion in Bajt, 1972).

Some simple tests supporting the thesis that after 1960 the Yugoslav cycles became true business cycles, were already provided by Bajt (1972). I shall not repeat them here. Instead, I shall approach the problem by exploiting the structure of the existing econometric models of the Yugoslav economy. I limit myself to models that in one period or other served to forecast economic activity for practical, not only academic, purposes. Let me first mention that all are of the Keynesian type, that is based on demand as a short term determinant of economic activity (for the best elaborated one see Bole and Mencinger, 1980). Since these are too large to be displayed here, I present one variant of a simple seven equation reduced form recursive model which clearly displays all the elements relevant to our discussion. First, as the main (in fact the only) determinants of economic activity, as proxied by industrial output, we find consumption (separately personal and public) and investment demand. Since in the traditional Keynesian theory only autonomous expenditures determine changes in economic activity, only autonomous consumption and autonomous investment are included. Following the standard theory of induced and autonomous demand, the

14

former are proxied by the residuals of a private (1) and a public (5) consumption function, and the latter by an accelerator type investment function (3). Empirically, both autonomous consumption and investment, as defined in the model, lead economic activity for several months. Thus forecasting is carried out by using autonomous expenditures as leading indicators. Secondly, no supply factors, i.e. a production function showing the dependence of economic activity on capital and employment, is included in the model. Whenever I tried to include them, their contribution was invariably insignificantly different from zero.

I present this model exactly in the form in which it appeared in Bajt, 1974. It is estimated for 1960-73, by OLS, for monthly data. For practical uses it was re-estimated for each run and several alternative specifications. Its practical use stretches from 1968 to 1980, when import constraints became decisive for the course of the economy. Throughout this period its performance was outstanding. Forecasts were not only produced for the Federal Government; my forecasts of the Yugoslav developments for Wharton Associate, Inc. World surveys (published in Newsweek and Business Week) were also based on this model.

$$CPD_t = -119.85 + 0.879\,Y_t$$
$$\quad\quad\quad\;\;(-5.1)\quad\;\;(214.8)$$
$$R^2 = 0.996,\ T = 49 - 214 \tag{1}$$

$$CPA = CP/CPD - 1 \tag{2}$$

$$ID_t = 900.67 + 1.610\,(CP_{t-1} - CP_{t-13})$$
$$\quad\quad\;\;(18.1)\quad\;\;(33.1)$$
$$R^2 = 0.87,\ T = 49 - 210 \tag{3}$$

$$IA = ID/I - 1 \tag{4}$$

$$GD_t = 146.4 + 0.171\,Y_t$$
$$\quad\quad\;\;(7.4)\quad\quad(47) \tag{5}$$

$$GA = GD/G - 1 \tag{6}$$

$$rQ_t = 10.9 + 55.9\,CPA_{t-9} + 11.1\,IA_{t-7} + 10.1\,GA_{t-5} - 0.023\,T \tag{7}$$
$$\quad\;(8.3)\quad(9.7)\quad\quad\;\;(5.8)\quad\quad\;(6.3)\quad\quad\;(2.5)$$
$$R^2 = 0.57,\ T = 58 - 214$$

All nominal values (CP = private expenditure on goods, I = investment expenditures on fixed and working capital, G = public-Government expenditures, federal, republican and local, Y = disposable personal incomes) are in millions of current dinars. Q is economic activity as measured by the index of industrial production (mining and energy included), $100 = \emptyset\ 1972$. D and A added to the above symbols stand for derived and autonomous, respectively, and r for monthly rate of growth.

The fit of equation (7) is very satisfactory, if one considers that it is for monthly rates of growth (trended data). For instance, $R^2$ of the consumption function (1), when estimated for monthly rates, amounts to only 0.37.

It is easy to see that the above model exploits the causal analysis presented in the preceding section, but with one difference. Autonomous expenditures defined as residuals of the corresponding behavioural function are not used to estimate the degree and direction of causation between variables of the same equation, but are, assuming causal dependence of economic activity on autonomous expenditures, brought into the economic activity equation as independent variables (7).

The results of the above model corroborate our finding that in Yugoslavia investment is more likely to be dependent on output than viceversa. Only to the extent that it is autonomous does investment influence economic activity. Furthermore, our model shows that not only investment but, as in other market economies, consumption as well, both private and public, is powerful, compared with investment. Again, consumption also appears as a determinant of economic activity only to the extent that it is autonomous.

This allows us to conclude that the Yugoslav cycles in economic activity during the period for which the above version of our model is estimated (1960-73) and also during the period for which it was used (1968-80), although in slightly different specifications and different structure, were indeed business cycles, that is demand and not capacity generated. The capacity generated investment cycles from the fifties were in the sixties and seventies transformed into business cycles, or, perhaps more correctly, the former were submerged by the latter.

Two observations appear to be warranted. First, one may ask why the same model has not been estimated for the 1947-60 period. For this period expected values of accelerator and marginal propensities (private and public) should not be significantly different from zero. The only reason is unavailability of data. Monthly data on the relevant variables exist only from January 1956 onwards. The period 1956-60 is too short to provide reliable estimates. Moreover, as argued above, demand was at least *co* shaping the pace of the economy even in that period.

Second, the reader may have noticed that while the estimate of the accelerator in (3) is a plausible one, lying in the field of damped oscillations (Samuelson, 1939), the sum of the two marginal propensities to consume in (1) and (5) alone drives the economy into increasingly larger instability. While this corresponds to real trends in Yugoslav economy, in the above model consumption and investment equations are estimated only to obtain proxies for autonomous expenditure. However, neither accelerator nor multiplier as such influence the course of the economy in the above model.

## On the relevance of the Yugoslav macro experience for other socialist countries

Our finding that Yugoslav economic reforms fundamentally changed the macro mechanism of her economy, raises the question of whether and how relevant the Yugoslav experience may be for other socialist countries. Needless to say, our interest is limited to the real sector only. Monetary instability falls beyond the scope of this paper.

Although we did not discuss the relative merits of decentralisation in economic decision making and of the corresponding marketisation of the economy on the one hand, and of self-management on the other, the former and not the latter appears to be decisive in the described transformation process. While self-management did contribute to greater independence of enterprises, independent enterprises are imaginable also without self-management. That is, with reforms which decentralise economic decision making, assuming they are far-reaching enough and successful, other socialist countries may also experience a transformation of their economic mechanism from capacity to demand determined. In this way, they may also get rid of investment cycles, but may find themselves faced with the emergence of business cycles of even greater intensity.

Reminding socialist reformers of the possibility that, through their efforts, minor problems with investment cycles, almost mastered by now, may be traded for major problems with business cycles, not successfully mastered even in capitalist countries, is not meant to discourage them. Decentralisation of the economy, its marketisation, is not desirable for its macro economic advantages, e.g. for abolition of investment cycles. It is needed in order to improve the allocative efficiency of the economy, to increase labour effort, both physical and intellectual, but above all to stimulate technical progress which, without market evaluation, is simply not possible. Macro-effects of decentralisation, that is instability of growth, have to be regarded as a byproduct. If they are unexpected, and catch reformers by surprise, it may induce them to overreact, and retreat from reforms.

An early warning that business cycles may accompany decentralisation of their economies, should induce socialist reformers to design macrostabilisation policies in advance. They enjoy two advantages, compared with capitalist countries. First, a large literature on stabilisation problems has been accumulated over the years in the West. This kind of technical progress is available free. Second, while the existing macro-control mechanisms in the East conflict with the market type economy, they could be retained during a transitional period, needed for introduction of efficient demand-management techniques.

However, the most relevant Yugoslav experience with economic reforms does not derive from their macro-effects. All socialist economic reforms so far, the Yugoslav included, have allowed markets to operate in the product sector, and only to a limited degree. Typically only consumer goods markets have been introduced, in order to equilibrate supply and demand. Almost complete physical control was retained over factors, comprising not only primary factors but also means of production, raw and other materials together with capital equipment. In other words, whether they were aware of it or not, by marketisation of the economy the reformers meant introduction of Lange's type of market socialism. In Lange's (1936) model only product prices are determined by the market. All factor prices are set by central planners who use modern optimisation techniques. With electronic computers, which enjoy 'an unchallenged superiority', compared with markets, simulation of equilibrium prices becomes a very simple task (Lange, 1967). This, however, is a fundamental mistake. If reforms are limited to product markets, or even to consumer goods markets, they can result in only marginal improvements. Since they are almost bound to expose the economy to demand generated macro-instability, the overall effects are likely to be negative on balance. Yugoslavia serves as a classical example. If decentralisation of economic decision making and marketisation is to increase efficiency of socialist economic systems, it has to be applied to products *and* factors, above all to capital and labour. This, however, makes superfluous not only central planners but the existing political elites as well. Radical political reforms appear to be a precondition for successful reforms. Since they conflict with the inherent interests of political elites, economic reforms are not likely to be far-reaching enough to guarantee success.

# References

Akademija nauk SSR (1958), *Politiceskaja ekonomija*, Ucebnik (Political economy — A textbook), Third edition, Moscow.

Bajt, A. (1971), 'Investment cycles in European socialist countries: A review article', *The Journal of Economic Literature*, no. 9, pp. 53-63.

— (1972), 'Le fluttuazioni cicliche nelle economie socialiste del dopoguerra, Piano e moneta nelle economie dell'Est', CESES, *Quaderni de l'Est*, no. 1, Milano, pp. 151-196 (plus 7 figures).

— (1974), 'Pattern of instability in socialist countries: Do they call for internationally coordinated stabilization measures?', *International Aspects of Stabilization Policies*, FRB of Boston and ISPE, Boston, pp. 357-380.

— (1984), 'Una riconsiderazione dello sviluppo economico jugoslavo', *Rivista di Politica Economica*, n. 74, Serie III, pp. 231-59.

Bauer, T. (1978), 'Investment cycles in Planned economies', *Acta Œconomica*, no. 21, pp. 243-260.

Bole, V. and Mencinger, J. (1980), *Ekonometricni model jugoslovanskega gospodarstva* (Econometric Model of the Yugoslav Economy), EIPF, Ljubljana.

Cobeljic, N. and Stojanovic, R. (1966), *Teorija investicionih ciklusa u socialistickoj privredi* (The theory of investment cycles in a socialist economy), IER, Belgrade (also published in *Eastern European Economics*, 1968-69, no. 7 (1-2).

Dallago, B. (1980), 'Cicli e fluttuazioni nelle economie socialiste: una rassegna delle principali interpretazioni', *Est-Ovest,* no. 11, pp. 95-122.

Domar, E.D. (1947), 'Expansion and Employment', *American Economic Review*, no. 37, pp. 34-55.

Fallenbuchl, Z.M. (1984), 'L'interaction de la stratégie de développement et du système économique, source de crises socio-économiques periodiques en Pologne', *Revue d'études comparatives Est-Ouest*, no. 15, pp. 113-130.

Frateschi, C. (1980), 'Sviluppo economico e instabilità nel dopoguerra: Un confronto tra alcuni paesi capitalisti e socialisti', *Est-Ovest*, n. 11, pp. 65-93.

Haavelmo, T. (1948), 'The statistical implication of a system of simultaneous equations', *Econometrica*, no. 11, pp. 1-12.

Horvat, B. (1969), *Privredni ciklusi u Jugoslaviji* (Economic Cycles in Yugoslavia), IER, Belgrad (also in English as *Business Cycles in Yugoslavia*, IASP, New York, 1970).

Kendall, G.M. (1946), *Studies in Oscillatory Time Series*, Cambridge.

Klotz, B. (1971), *Do planners make Waves?* An unpublished comment on Bajt, 1971.

Kornai, J. (1986), 'The Hungarian reform process: Visions, Hopes, and Reality', *Journal of Economic Literature*, no. 24, pp. 1687-1737.

Lange, O. (1937), 'On the economic theory of socialism', *Review of Economic Studies*, no. 4, pp. 53-71 and 123-142.

Lange, O. (1967), 'The computer and the market' in Feinstein,C.H. (ed.) *Socialism, Capitalism and Economic Growth: Essays Presented to Maurice Dobb*, , Cambridge, pp. 158-61.

Nove, A. (1986), 'Contribution de la tecnologie importée à la croissance sovietique', *Revue d'études comparatives Est-Ouest*, no. 17, pp. 21-32.

Olivera, J. (1960), 'Cyclical economic growth under collectivism', *Kyklos*, no. 13, pp. 229-55.

Roman, Z. (1985), 'Productivity growth and its slowdown in the Hungarian economy', *Acta Œconomica*, no. 35, pp. 81-104.

Sargent, T.J. (1978), 'Rational expectations, econometric exogeneity, and consumption', *Journal of Political Economy*, no. 86, pp. 673-700.

Sims, C.A. (1972), 'Money, income, and causality', *American Economic Review*, no. 62, pp. 540-52.

Samuelson, P. (1939), 'Interactions between the multiplier and the principle of accelerator', *Review of Economic Statistics*, no. 21, pp. 75-78.

Schrettl, W. (1983), *Consumption, Efforts, and Growth in Soviet-type Economies: a Theoretical Analysis*, a facsimile edition by U.M.I., Ann Arbor, Michigan.

Soòs, A. (1978), 'Some general problems of the Hungarian investment system', *Acta Œconomica*, no. 21, pp. 223-242.

# 2 Macroeconomic instability and cycles in Czechoslovakia

CARLO FRATESCHI

## Introduction

The paper deals with the problem of macroeconomic instability and cyclical fluctuations in Czechoslovakia. The first part examines the evolution of some macroeconomic aggregates in the 1950-1985 period: their pattern of growth and the measurement of their instability show a certain number of stylised facts that should be taken into consideration in an analysis of postwar economic growth in Czechoslovakia.

In the second part, which deals more in particular with the fluctuation in industrial output, it emerges not only a clear pulsating pattern of growth but a surprisingly regular five-year cycle (especially in the after-1965 period): from 1966 onwards the growth rate of Net Industrial Production shows a trough in the second year of every five-year planning period, while the corresponding peaks have occurred twice in the last, one in the fourth and once in the third year of the planning period. A rather regular cycle is also identified in the evolution of the 'degree of plan fulfillment' (both for Industrial Production and for Total Investment Outlays).

The third part of the paper examines the relationship between Output and Investment, and arrives at the following conclusions: a) the fluctuations in the growth rates of Net Industrial Output depend in a very significant measure on the growth rates of Investment outlays in the preceding year; b) this dependence has to be attributed predominantly to the effect of the variable degree of fulfillment of investment plans, and only in a minor way to the effect of the variation in the planned growth rates of investment; c) the causation running from investment to output seems to derive more from the 'demand effect' of investment on production than from the 'capacity effect' of new investment goods put into operation.

The fourth and last part of the paper deals with the evolution of an important variable: the ratio of the value of investment projects started during each year over the value of investment projects completed in the same year. This ratio constitutes a crucial indicator because it records very carefully the variation in the degree of tension in the investment sphere. From the analysis it emerges a clear and definite cyclical character in the timing of this indicator, which follows almost strictly a five-year pattern. Moreover, the increase in unfinished construction, another typical "shortage" indicator, is shown to exhibit a similar pattern.

## Total economic instability: patterns and measures

Our main objective is to show a certain number of stylised facts that one should take into consideration and try to explain in an analysis of postwar economic instability and cycles in Czechoslovakia. This being the aim, the obvious starting point is the evolution of the growth rates of total net material product.

Looking at Fig. 2.1 it seems plausible first of all to distinguish two phases. The first, 1950-1965, is composed of a ten year period of damped fluctuations around a 7% average growth rate and a subsequent deep and long recession that lasts for about three years. In the second phase, 1966-1985, the picture is slightly different: again damped fluctuations for about ten years, around a 6% average, followed by a progressive slowdown that culminates in a somewhat milder recession, compared to the 1963 crisis, at the beginning of the 1980s.

Since part of the macro instability could be connected to the extremely strong and to a certain extent exogenous short-run fluctuations of agricultural production, we can look in Figure 2.2 at the Net Material Product exclusive of agriculture.

The general picture does not change very much, the only major difference being that during the 1950s this series exhibits higher rates of growth, around an 8% average, and an exceptional stability from 1958 to 1961.

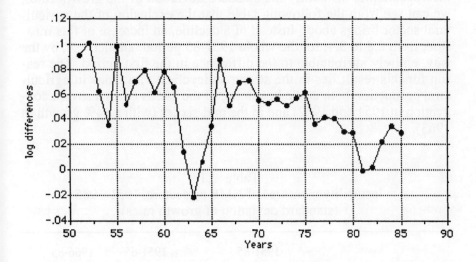

Figure 2.1 Annual growth rates of Total Net Material Product

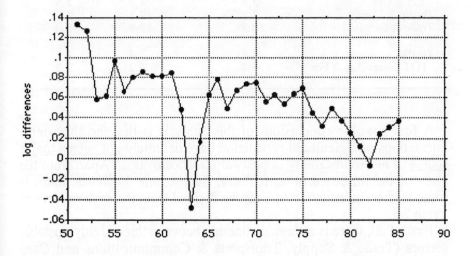

Figure 2.2 Annual growth rates of Net Material Product <u>except</u> for the sector 'Agriculture and Forestry'

To infer from this evidence that the fluctuations in agricultural production contributed significantly to macroeconomic instability would be, however, incorrect. In fact, if we take as a measure of macroeconomic instability the standard deviation of the growth rates, we can see from the following table that the exclusion of the agricultural sector brings about, instead of a decline, an increase of this measure, from 2.8 to 3.4, for the whole 1951-85 period: an increase, by the way, entirely attributable to the difference in the first period. The reason for this result lies in the strong anticyclical variations in agricultural production both at the beginning of the 1950s (with a severe contraction in 1951 and 1952) and in the mid-sixties (with a 14% growth in 1963).

Table 2.1
Instability measures of NMP by sectors, 1951-1985
(standard deviation of growth rates)

|  | 1951-85 | 1951-65 | 1966-85 |
| --- | --- | --- | --- |
| Agric & For | 8,6 | 9,2 | 7,5 |
| Industry | 3,5 | 4,1 | 2,4 |
| Construction | 8,4 | 11,0 | 5,0 |
| Ind & Const | 3,8 | 4,5 | 2,5 |
| Transp & Comm | 7,2 | 9,1 | 3,8 |
| Trade & Supply | 10,3 | 12,9 | 5,0 |
| Total | 2,8 | 3,4 | 2,1 |
| TOT except Agr & For | 3,4 | 4,2 | 2,2 |

A first possible conclusion of this analysis is that the short-term fluctuations of agricultural production have definitely not been a major source of macro instability in postwar Czechoslovakia. Apart from the issue of the influence of agricultural fluctuations, however, there is some further information that can be derived from the sectoral data of Table 2.1.

First of all, there is a sharp distinction between three highly unstable sectors (Trade & Supply, Transports & Communications and Construction) and Industry. But these same sectors ('material services' and construction) show a significant reduction in the amplitude of their fluctuations, more than halving their instability between the first and the second period: this results in a significant narrowing in the range of sectoral instability measures.

Secondly, in every period there is no single sector in which the instability of growth rates appears to be lower than the instability for the whole economy. This indicates that the fluctuations in growth rates have not been always and completely pervasive. In fact, the following Figure 2.3 shows in particular that while there is a relatively high degree of concordance (=a low standard deviation of growth rates) in most of the 'high growth' years of the first period (1955, 1958, 1961, 1965), in the 'bad years' the intersectoral dispersion tends to grow (1956, 1964, 1977, 1982). There are exceptions to this 'rule', the most notable being the 1963 situation:a bad year, indeed the worst, in which the intersectoral dispersion of growth rates is comparatively low.

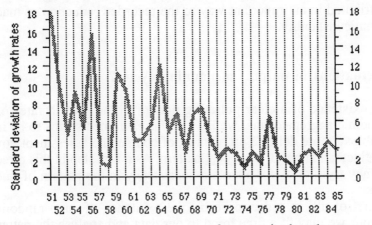

Figure 2.3 Dispersion of growth rates of non-agricultural sectors

But this is exactly the reason why the 1963 crisis was so severe: all the economic sectors, the only exception being agriculture, experienced negative growth rates.

This pattern of alternate high and low intersectoral co-variation, respectively during the acceleration and the deceleration years, may therefore yield some interesting insights into the fluctuation generating mechanism. The fact that at the peak of the expansion the different economic sectors tend to 'grow together' makes a strong contribution to that overheating of the economic situation which, in the context of a centrally planned economy, generates growing disproportions and shortages and creates the conditions for the subsequent slowdown. On the other hand, the emergence at the bottom of the cycle of a certain

<u>disconnection</u> of the sectoral growth rates has two important consequences: it helps to mitigate the depth of the recession at the global level, thanks to the anticlycical behaviour of some sectors, and it probably tends to shorten the length of the slowdown, since at the microlevel this relative difference of speed may contribute to an improvement of the supply situation, a smoothing of interindustry and interfirm relationships and to the setting in motion of a certain dishoarding of stocks.

This asymmetric behaviour seems to hold, it must be noted, only for the period 1951-65: in the second phase, in fact, the peaks of the output cycle do not correspond to the troughs of the dispersion indicator. This fact could indicate that after 1965 at least one of the causes of the overstraining of the economy typical of the booms, the coincidence of sectoral high growth rates, partially disappeared: this change may have contributed in an important way to the recorded reduction of macroeconomic instability.


## Fluctuations in output: a planning cycle ?

The existence of a clear pulsating pattern in the growth rates of the economic aggregates that we have so far examined seems to be indisputable: a more delicate problem is, of course, the assessment not just of a fluctuating but of a <u>cyclical</u> pattern. As a first step in this direction we may try to look for a certain consistency in the pattern of fluctuations.

First of all, in order to verify the existence of non-random behaviour we may fit a time trend to our data and analyse the pattern of the deviations from this trend: in particular, if we verify the existence of a positive serial correlation in residuals, we may infer that we are in the presence not just of an alternating movement but of a cyclical pattern.

By fitting a second-degree polynomial time trend to the logarithmic differences of the non-agricultural Net Material Product, we obtain for the Durbin-Watson '$d$' statistics a value of 1.16, significative at the 0.05 level: consequently we may accept the existence of a first-order autocorrelation of residuals and, hence, of some sort of cyclical pattern in aggregate economic fluctuations. From an analysis of the residuals shown in Fig. 2.3 it is possible, moreover, to better identify the upper and lower turning points of this wave-like movement.

The only uncertainty, as far as the determination of the turning points is concerned, regards the identification of the 1971 minor slow-

26

# Table 2.2
## Turning points, and length of acceleration and deceleration phases, of cycles in non-agricultural Net Material Product

| PEAKS: | 1951 | | 1955 | | 1961 | | 1966 | | 1970(?) | | 1975 | | 1978 | | 1985 |
|---|---|---|---|---|---|---|---|---|---|---|---|---|---|---|---|
| Length of | | 2 | | 4 | | 3 | | 3 | | 4 | | 1 | | 3 | |
| phases | 2 | | 2 | | 2 | | 1 | | 1 | | 2 | | 4 | | |
| TROUGHS: | | 1953 | | 1957 | | 1963 | | 1967 | | 1971(?) | | 1977 | | 1982 | |

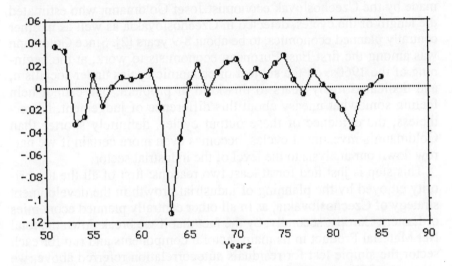

Figure 2.3    Deviations from trend of non-agricultural NMP

down as a minimum in the cycle. By accepting it, even if it does not stand out clearly as a trough with respect to the fitted trend, we obtain a series of fluctuations of irregular amplitude but of a well defined and regular periodicity. The length of the successive cycles, as measured at the turning points, is as follows:

4,6,5,4,5,3,7 years     = average of 4.9 years from peak to peak
4,6,4,4,6,5    years     = average of 4.8 years from trough to trough

Moreover, each cycle also exhibits a quite regular time pattern, with an acceleration phase of 3 or 4 years (the most notable exception being the very short one from 1977 to 1978) and a slowdown phase of the length of 2 years or 1 (again with the exception of the long slackening from 1978 to 1982).

As we said above, the amplitude of these cycles, on the contrary, does not show any regularity. In terms of deviations from the trend there is in fact a great variation, ranging from the extremely serious 1963 crisis (-11 percentage points), to the clear recessions of 1953 and 1982 (about -4 % points), to the mild slowdowns of 1957, 1967, 1971 and 1977.

As already noted by Gerritse in his excellent and well argumented dissertation [1], the existence of these five-year cycles is in sharp contrast to the observations regarding the duration of the socialist cycle made by the Czechoslovak economist Josef Goldmann, who estimated the length of the cycles, detected in Czechoslovakia as well as in other centrally planned economies, to be about 8-9 years [2]. Since Goldmann was among the first East European economists to work, at the beginning of the 1960s, on the subject of economic cycles under socialism, and dedicated many years to this kind of problem, one cannot help feeling somewhat uneasy about this difference of judgement. Nevertheless, the evidence of these output cycles, definitely shorter than Goldmann's investment cycles, becomes even more certain if we narrow down our analysis to the level of the industrial sector.

This step is justified for at least two reasons: first of all the top priority enjoyed by the planning of industrial growth in the development strategy of Czechoslovakia, as in all other centrally planned economies of Eastern Europe; secondly, by the fact that if we break down the total Net Material Product in its main sectoral components and run for each sector the simple test for residuals autocorrelation referred above, we obtain the following results:

*Durbin Watson 'd'*

| | |
|---|---|
| Agriculture and Forestry | 2.9 |
| Industry | 1.22 |
| Construction | 1.66 |
| Transport and Communications | 2.18 |
| Trade and Material Supply | 1.7 |

There is no doubt, at least according to this test, that the only sector for which we can speak with an acceptable degree of confidence of a first-order positive correlation of residuals is Industry. For Construction, Transport and Trade we have to accept the null hypothesis of no

<u>autocorrelation</u>, while for Agriculture we obtain a value that indicates a first-order <u>negative</u> autocorrelation of residuals (a result by no means unexpected, since it corresponds to a pattern of extremely short-term, year to year oscillation, not very different from the observed fluctuations of agricultural production).

From the following Figure 2.4 we can easily identify the turning points of the industrial cycle:

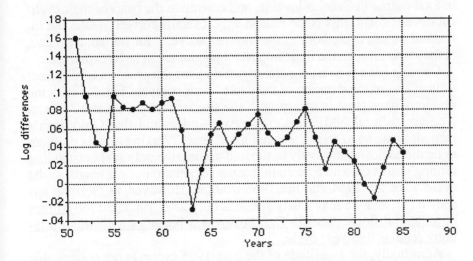

Figure 2.4   Growth rates (log differences) of Net Material Product created in Industry

Table 2.3
Turning points, and length of acceleration and deceleration phases, of cycles in  Net Material Product created in Industry

| PEAKS: | 1951 | | 1955 | | 1961 | | 1966 | | 1970 | | 1975 | | 1978 | | 1984 |
|---|---|---|---|---|---|---|---|---|---|---|---|---|---|---|---|
| Length of phases | | 1 | | 4 | | 3 | | 3 | | 3 | | 1 | | 2 | |
| | 3 | | 2 | | 2 | | 1 | | 2 | | 2 | | 4 | | |
| TROUGHS: | | 1954 | | 1957 | | 1963 | | 1967 | | 1972 | | 1977 | | 1982 | |

By comparing Table 2.3 with Table 2.2, we observe a complete correspondence in the turning points, with the only minor exceptions of two troughs (1954 and 1972 instead of 1953 and 1971) and one peak

29

(1984 instead of 1985). Obviously, the length of each cycle, as well as the average, is still almost the same:

4,6,5,4,5,3,6  years = average of 4.7  years from peak to peak
3,6,4,5,5,5    years = average of 4.7  years from trough to trough

From a statistical point of view, in other words, the wave-like movements of industrial production seem to dominate the fluctuations in total output in Czechoslovakia, and constitute the basis of their cyclical development: this is the reason why it seems correct to take the industrial output cycle both as the 'reference cycle' for our analysis and, at the same time, as the most important phenomenon to be explained.

Coming back to what we already said about the problem of different estimations of the duration of the cycle, if we compare Fig. 2.4 with the previous ones (that is to say with the fluctuations in Total NMP and Non-agricultural NMP) we may easily understand that Goldmann's misjudgment, so to speak, was not a real one. Working on this problem as he did almost exclusively in the mid-sixties, the only real outstanding turning points on which he could base an evaluation of the length of the cycle were the 1954 and the 1963 troughs. However, as Gerritse has shown [3], and we may easily see, it is only after 1965 that the pattern of industrial fluctuations in Czechoslovakia becomes a clear, surprisingly regular five-year cycle.

Admittedly, the amplitude of the post-1965 cycles is not comparable to the big swings in growth rates that characterised the first half of the fifties and sixties. On the other hand, a regular cycle with an amplitude of 4 to 6 percentage points cannot be easily dismissed for lack of relevance: it represents, to say the least, an interesting phenomenon deserving further investigation.

The first striking characteristic of this pattern of fluctuations is, in fact, its regular periodicity. Many of the authors who have worked on the problem of cyclical fluctuations, both in centrally planned and in capitalist economies, share the view that, in order to identify a cycle, a strict and regular periodicity is not needed [4]. But regularity, even if it is not a necessary condition, can be considered at least as a serious symptom of an underlying cyclical process. In particular, one has to take into consideration the fact that from 1966 onwards the fluctuations in the growth rate of net industrial production show a trough in the second year of every five-year planning period, while the corresponding peaks occurred twice in the last, once in the fourth and once in the third year of the planning period. It is of a certain interest, moreover, that this pattern fits perfectly with the following description:

30

'There is a planning cycle in the growth of industrial production in the Soviet economy, which is caused by the periodicity of the long-term (regularly five-year) national economic plans and by the simultaneous effects of the incentive system, the ratchet principle and the tautness of planning, which are inherent in the Soviet system of enterprise administration. The variation in the rate of growth caused by these factors and the resultant planning cycle have a fairly stable relationship to the long-term planning periods. There is a trough in the volume of production at the beginning of the period (the first and the second year of the five-year period) and a peak in the latter half of the period (the fourth or fifth year of the five-year period).'[5]

In this passage the author, after a long analysis of the planning mechanism in the Soviet economy, especially at the enterprise level, summarises his theoretical findings and states the hypotheses that he subsequently intends to test. However the verification, carried out by Dahlstedt for the Soviet Union, fits the theoretical model only partially, in the sense that the timing of the hypothesised peaks and troughs does not correspond completely to the empirically observed one. On the contrary, as we have seen, in the case of post-1965 Czechoslovakia there is an almost absolute correspondence with the expected time pattern: since this is not, obviously, a mere coincidence, a further examination of Dahlstedt's model is more than warranted.

The starting point of his analysis, also built upon previous work by Hutchings [6], is a certain degree of dissatisfaction with some aspects of the previous work on cyclical fluctuations in centrally planned economies. More precisely, the apparent discrepancy between some of the observations made by economists working on this topic brings him to the conclusion that it is possible that under a common label of 'investment cycles' different authors may have in fact analysed different phenomena [7]. The possible, attempted solution consists in the elaboration of a 'planning cycle', defined as a

'..cyclical fluctuation which has its origin in the sequential periodicity of the long-term administrative planning and plan implementation. The cycle length is determined simultaneously. The role of investments is to be a part of the production process to implement the investment plan, that is, the construction of industrial, commercial and agricultural projects.' [8].

31

This 'planning cycle' model, centred upon a microeconomic analysis of managerial behaviour, is built on the interaction between the ratchet effect, with its negative impact on the degree of plan fulfilment, and taut planning. The main conclusion of the model, that depends crucially on the characteristics of the managers' success indicators, is that in the Soviet economy a steady-state growth is not, from the managerial point of view, the optimal solution: instead, a better time path is represented by a first phase of underfulfilment and a second phase of overfulfilment [9].

We do not have, of course, the possibility of testing at the enterprise level this specific hypothesis about the degree of under- and overfulfilment: what follows is a very crude test, at the level of macroeconomic aggregates. We examine and compare the time pattern of the planned and actual rates of growth of industrial production in Czechoslovakia, and by simply subtracting the second from the first we derive the 'degree of fulfilment', (positive or negative) of industrial output plans.

Due to some time limitations in the series we can only start from 1954: but the most important point to stress is that in this case we are not dealing, as we have till now, with value added data on Net Industrial Product (more precisely, Net Material Product created in Industry) but with the index of Gross Industrial Production: it is only with respect to this aggregate that it is possible to reconstruct long-term series on planned and realised rates of growth.

First of all it must be underlined that the cycles in Net and Gross Industrial Production do not share an identical time pattern. If we compare the upper and lower turning points in the 'REALISED IND PROD' graph with the troughs and peaks of Net Industrial Product (Table 2.3) we can make the following observations:

a) there is a perfect coincidence as far as the most severe recessions are concerned: 1954, 1963, 1982;
b) as to the peaks, they coincide in four cases: 1955, 1970, 1975, 1984;
c) in three other cases there seems to exist a <u>lead</u> of gross over net output: one trough, 1956 instead of 1957, two peaks, 1960 and 1965 instead of 1961 and 1966;
d) in two troughs there is, apparently, a two-year <u>lag</u>: 1969 instead of 1967 and 1974 instead of 1972;
e) finally, there are no clearly discernible turning points between the 1975 peak and the 1982 trough (instead of a 1977 trough and a 1978 peak).

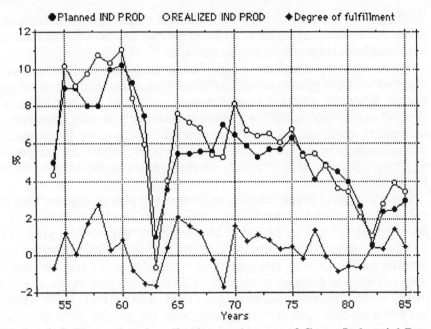

Figure 2.5 Planned and realised growth rates of Gross Industrial Production (in %).

We have gone through this rather detailed comparison for two main reasons. The first one relates to the possible general implications of this difference in timing. This phenomenon was observed and analysed for the first time, as far as we know, by Gerritse, who places a great emphasis on the two-year lag in troughs that we have showed in 1969 and 1974 : in fact he presupposes the existence of one more case of a two-year lag, because working with data that extend only to 1979 he is led to assume, mistakenly, that the 1979 low growth rate was a lower turning point. Consequently, some theoretical explanations are put forward for this 'lagging troughs of the gross industrial output cycle' phenomenon [10].

While we fully agree with Gerritse on the importance of clearly distinguishing between cycles in net value added and in gross production, in order at least to avoid ambiguities and undesirable confusion, his characterisation of the 'Gross Output Cycle' as showing in general a two-year lag in troughs (with respect to the Net output cycle) does not seem to be well grounded: after all, by looking for instance at the period 1954-66 one could also speak of a pattern characterised by 'leading turning points of the gross industrial output cycle'. Or at least, to put it another way, what is to be explained is also this reversal in leads and lags, respectively before and after 1966.

There is a second and more specific reason, however, for the attention that we have paid to the differences between Net and Gross output cycles. Since, as we have seen, the time pattern of the Net Material Product in Industry exhibits a striking correspondence with Dahlstedt's theoretical 'planning cycle', we run into difficulty if we try to verify this hypothesis by means of an aggregate whose fluctuations are partly different. Bearing this in mind, we may return to the inspection of Figure 2.5.

From the lower graph, indeed, an alternating pattern appears also in the degree of plan fulfilment: the amplitude of the 'fulfilment cycle', fairly stable for a long period at about 4 percentage points around a mean close to zero (precisely O.4), seems to shrink a little from the beginning of the 1970's. The pattern is also sufficiently regular, but it does not seem to coincide completely with the gross output cycle: some of the turning points do correspond (1963, 1965, 1969, 1970, 1984) but some do not. As a matter of fact, from the graphs there does not emerge a regular sequence of underfulfilment in the first years of the five-year plans and overfulfilment in the last ones, as in Dahlstedt's hypothesis: but this result is not unexpected, since as we said it would not have much sense to search for this pattern with respect to a series that has a different timing.

## Cycles in plan-fulfilment and the investment-output nexus

The very rough test that we have conducted has not allowed us to verify the 'planning cycle hypothesis': however, it cannot be inferred from it that we should reject it, but rather that a better way to prove it should be looked for. One possible direction for future work should be, for instance, the analysis of sectoral data instead of aggregate data.

However, from the data on planned and actual rates of growth we may extract, in fact, some more interesting pieces of information, for instance a measure of the 'degree of control' that the planners exercise on the growth path of the economy. In order to do so, we can estimate a regression with the actual rates of growth as the dependent variable and the planned ones as the independent variable. In the case, so to speak, of perfect plan implementation we should obtain a perfect fit: on the contrary, a zero correlation between planned and actual rates of growth would be a sign of a complete lack of control over the economy by the planners.

This exercise has been performed not only for Gross Industrial Production but also for the series of planned and actual Total Investment Outlays, both for the total period and for two sub-periods (1954-65 and 1966-85). The results are summarised in Table 2.4. In the equations, $IND_t$ and $INV_t$ represent the values of the <u>actual</u> rates of growth of Industrial Production and Total Investment for each year, while $PIND_t$ and $PINV_t$ are the respective <u>planned</u> rates of growth.

Looking, first of all, at the values of the adjusted $R^2$, we are able to give a first numerical answer to the question regarding the degree of control of the planners over the economy. For example, in the case of Industry we obtain for the whole 1954-85 period the value of 0.85: in other words, 85% of the variance of the actual rates of growth is 'explained' by the variance in <u>planned</u> rates of growth. If we look at it the other way around, it means that in the last thirty years only 15% of the growth of industrial production has escaped the control (and the forecasts) of the central planners: since they are human beings, and consequently not omniscient or omnipotent, this may be judged, so to speak, quite a good score.

It should also be noted, however, that by looking at the sub-periods we are able to detect a worsening of the performance: in fact, for the period 1966-1985 the equation 'explains' only 75% of the variance in growth rates, which means that the planners did not control (or forecast) 25% of the variation in the growth of industry. Again, it is difficult to judge whether this particular value is, by itself, high or low: it would be interesting, for that matter, to do the same exercise for other centrally planned economies and make a cross-country comparison.

For Czechoslovakia we have in fact a touchstone, represented by Investment regression: by comparison with output planning, indeed, the score on investment planning is definitely lower. For the whole period the value of the adjusted $R^2$ is 0.58, which is the same as saying that in Czechoslovakia the central planning organs controlled <u>not much more than half of the variations in the growth of investment outlays</u>. On the other hand, there is an upward trend in the 'degree of control' between the first and the second sub-period: from O.54 to O.63, which amounts to a 9 points progress as opposed to a 9 points regress in the case of output planning. Even if this means that from 1966 onwards 37% of the variations in the growth rate of total investment still did not derive from the intention of central planners, the improvement is undoubtable.

Table 2.4
Regression relationships between planned and actual rates of growth
of Gross Industrial Production and Total Investment

| Period | Regression | Adj. $R^2$ | Std.Err. | t-value indep. var. | D.W. |
|--------|-----------|-----------|----------|---------------------|------|
| | **Gross Industrial Production** | | | | |
| 1954-85 | $IND_t = 0.026 + 1.067\ PIND_t$ | 0.85 | 1.1 | 13.3 | 1.42 |
| 1954-65 | $IND_t = -0.708 + 1.154\ PIND_t$ | 0.84 | 1.39 | 7.77 | 1.19 |
| 1966-85 | $IND_t = 0.475 + 0.985\ PIND_t$ | 0.753 | 0.93 | 7.68 | 1.73 |
| | **Total Investment Outlays** | | | | |
| 1954-85 | $INV_t = -0.047 + 0.886\ PIND_t$ | 0.58 | 4.16 | 6.39 | 1.36 |
| 1954-65 | $INV_t = -2.2 + 0.974\ PIND_t$ | 0.543 | 5.68 | 3.75 | 1.17 |
| 1966-85 | $INV_t = -0.119 + 1.115\ PIND_t$ | 0.633 | 2.77 | 5.66 | 2.11 |

The greater difficulties met in the planning of investment is re-
flected, obviously, also in the much higher values of the standard error
of estimate, a fact which we can further elaborate by inspecting Fig.
2.6, in which we have plotted the residuals of both our long-term
regressions. We may easily verify, first of all, the greater variability of
the investment residuals with respect to the output residuals, and at the
same time its reduction after 1965. Moreover, we can also see that
their cyclical time pattern, which represents of course the evolution of
the degree of underfulfilment and overfulfillment of investment plans,
shows the following turning points:

Table 2.5
Turning points, and length of acceleration and deceleration phases,of
cycles in the Degree of Fulfilment of Total Investment Outlays

| PEAKS: | 1955 | | 1959 | | 1966 | | 1969 | | 1974 | | 1977 | | 1983 | |
|--------|------|---|------|---|------|---|------|---|------|---|------|---|------|---|
| Length of | 1 | | 4 | | 1 | | 2 | | 2 | | 4 | | 1 | |
| phases | | 3 | | 3 | | 2 | | 3 | | 1 | | 2 | | |
| TROUGHS: | | 1956 | | 1963 | | 1967 | | 1971 | | 1976 | | 1981 | | 1984 |

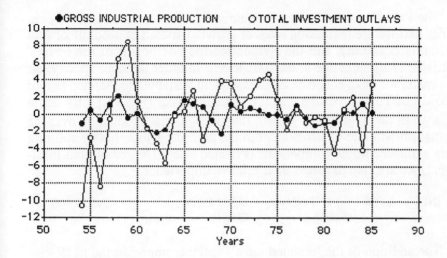

Figure 2.6 Residuals from a linear regression of actual over planned rates of growth

If we measure the length of each cycle, as well as their average, we obtain the following figures:

4,7,3,5,3,6   years = average of 4.7 years from peak to peak
7,4,4,5,5,3   years = average of 4.7 years from trough to trough

These results seem, indeed, rather remarkable: the average length is perfectly identical to the cycle in Net Industrial Product, while the timing of peaks and lags exhibits very striking characteristics, if compared with it. While in four cases, two peaks (1955, 1966) and two troughs (1963,1967) there is a correspondence, <u>in all other cases the turning points of the Fulfilment of Investment Plan cycle show a one year lead over the Industrial cycle</u> (except in 1959, when the lead is a two-year one). In fact, if we consider only the period after 1967, the one-year lead is the absolute rule in every turning point.

In order to better verify this particular relationship we ran a linear regression with the growth rates in Net Material Product in Industry $(IND_t)$ as the dependent variable and the values of the degree of fulfilment (= actual-planned growth rates) of Total Investment plan in the preceding year $(FPINV_{t-1})$ as the independent variable. For the period 1967-1985 we obtain the following estimate:

$$IND_t = 3.6 + 0.814 \ FPINV_{t-1} \qquad \text{Adj. } R^2 = 0.634$$
$$(5.195)$$

The value for the adjusted R-squared is a very good one, if we consider that we are regressing rates of growth (instead of absolute or logarithmised values), and the t-value for the coefficient of the FPINV variable is significative at the 0.01 level. In order to better specify our estimate, we have added as an independent variable the Planned rate of growth of Total Investment in the preceding year ($PINV_{t-1}$). By doing this we in fact regress the growth rate of Industrial Production over the actual growth rate of Investment in the preceding year: but by splitting this variable into its components (Planned rate + Degree of plan fulfilment) we are able to assess their relative importance:

$$IND_t = 2.794 + 0.743 \ FPINV_{t-1} + 0.232 \ PINV_{t-1} \qquad Adj. \ R^2 = 0.701$$
$$\qquad\qquad (5.095) \qquad\qquad (2.031)$$

The addition of the 'planned rates' variable improves the fit ($R^2$ increases to O.701), but its coefficient is lower than the coefficient of the 'fulfilment indicator', and its significance is acceptable only at the 0.05 level. The most important thing, however, is that even if we accept this second specification, the result seem to indicate the existence of the following kind of relationship: a) the growth rates of Net Industrial Product depend to significant degree on the growth rates of actual total investment outlays in the preceding year; b) this dependence has to be attributed predominantly to the effect of the variable degree of fulfilment of investment plans, and only in a minor way to the effect of variation in the planned growth rates of investment (the first variable being three times more important).

We may thus say with a sufficient degree of confidence that in Czechoslovakia, in the twenty years from 1967 to 1985, there is not only a positive correlation between investment and industrial output, but that the direction of causation goes from the first to the second: or, more precisely, from the unplanned part of the first to the second.

This conclusion seems to be sufficiently well grounded. In fact, if we try to estimate the same equation with no lags in the variables, that is if we use coincident variables, we obtain less significant results: a considerably lower coefficient of determination (O.446) and a not significant value for the coefficient of the 'plan fulfilment' variable.

$$IND_t = 2.091 + 0.227 \ FPINV_t + 0.511 \ PINV_t \qquad Adj. \ R^2 = 0.446$$
$$\qquad\qquad (1.204) \qquad\qquad (3.349)$$

Moreover, if we try to verify the opposite direction of causation, from output to investment, by using the growth rates of Total Investment as the dependent variable and the growth rates of Net Industrial Production in the preceding year as the explicative variable, the resulting estimate shows a weaker correlation (adj. $R^2 = 0.387$).

There are two different aspects in the question of the correlation between industrial production and investment. The first one is, as we said, the direction of the causal nexus: from investment to output or from output to investment. The second one is the kind of effect that we assume to exist between the variables. In particular, if we verify a causal nexus going from investment to output, as seems to be the case from the above estimations, we have two further possibilities: this link can be thought of as deriving from a demand effect (in fact a multiplier effect) of investment on production or, quite differently, from the capacity effect of new investment goods on production. This is, indeed, quite a controversial point among scholars. To throw some more light on this issue we have estimated a series of regressions between different variables: Total Investment, Industrial Investment, Gross Industrial Production, Net Industrial Product. All the regressions, estimated with O.L.S. for the period 1954-1985, have the form

$$X_t = a + b Y_t + c Y_{t-1} + u_t$$

and the results are summarised in Table 2.6.

To interpret the regression results one should bear in mind the fact that in the first group of equations (from eq. 1 to eq. 4) we estimated the amount of the variance in growth rates of Gross Industrial Production (1,2) or Net Industrial Product (3,4) explained by the growth rates of Total or Industrial Investment in the same year and in the preceding year. In the second group the reverse relationship has been estimated, that is to say the amount of the variance in growth rates of Total (5,6) or Industrial (7,8) Investment explained by the growth rates of Gross or Net industrial Production in the same year and in the preceding year. We use lags in independent variables as a means, albeit very crude, for identifying causal relationships.

The first conclusion which we can draw is that causation is mainly unidirectional. In the first group of equations the coefficients of the lagged variable are all significant: three of them at the 0.01 level, the fourth at the 0.05 level. On the contrary in the second group of equations, estimating the causal nexus going from Industrial Production to Investment, all the coefficients of the lagged variable are not significant, except in the first equation (at the 0.05 level). We may therefore exclude the second group of equations and concentrate on the first one.

## Table 2.6
### Regression relationships between Growth Rates of Gross Industrial Production (GRIND) or Net Industrial Product (NETIND) and Total Investment (ITOT) or Investment in Industry (IIND) 1954-1985

| | | Adj. $R^2$ | F | D.W. |
|---|---|---|---|---|

**Causation: from Investment to Industrial Production**

1  $GRIND_t = 3.536 + 0.263\ ITOT_t + 0.195\ ITOT_{t-1}$    0.748   47.03   1.26
              (5.647)     (4.221)

2  $GRIND_t = 4.396 + 0.187\ IIND_t + 0.135\ IIND_{t-1}$    0.483   15.48   1.09
              (3.639)     (2.873)

3  $NETIND_t = 2.446 + 0.247\ ITOT_t + 0.226\ ITOT_{t-1}$    0.628   27.22   1.34
              (3.923)     (3.610)

4  $NETIND_t = 3.437 + 0.205\ IIND_t + 0.102\ IIND_{t-1}$    0.346   9.21   1.22
              (3.190)     (1.738)

**Causation: from Industrial Production to Investment**

5  $ITOT_t = -3.765 + 2.1\ GRIND_t - 0.552\ GRIND_{t-1}$    0.631   27.53   2.10
              (6.566)     (1.725)

6  $ITOT_t = -0.676 + 0.164\ NETIND_t - 0.414\ NETIND_{t-1}$    0.491   15.97   1.65
              (5.182)     (1.302)

7  $IIND_t = -0.053 + 1.4\ GRIND_t + 0.4\ GRIND_{t-1}$    0.347   9.23   2.24
              (2.735)     (0.691)

8  $IIND_t = -0.23 + 1.124\ NETIND_t + 0.384\ NETIND_{t-1}$    0.491   15.97   1.65
              (2.514)     (0.855)

Once we have established that the changes in investment dominate the changes in production, we may try to assess if this linkage operates via demand or capacity effects: in order to do this, we may compare equations 1 and 3 with equations 2 and 4.

In fact, if the changes in industrial production were the result of a 'capacity effect' of new investment goods put into operation in industry, we should have in the estimated equation a stronger effect coming from Industrial Investment ($IIND_t$ and $IIND_{t-1}$) as opposed to Total Investment: this is a sensible hypothesis, we think, since only that part of Total Investment Outlays which pertains to Industry may have the effect of increasing productive capacity in industry.

On the other hand the opposite would be true (i.e. we would obtain a stronger correlation with Total Investment) if changes in the growth rates of industrial production were motivated by a 'demand effect', that is by the growth in total demand generated by an increase in Total Investment (as opposed to just Industrial Investment).

Indeed, by looking at the regressions results we see that it is precisely this second interpretation that has to be accepted. Equation 1, in fact, shows much higher values for the coefficient of determination and the F-value (0.748 and 47.03) compared to Equation 2 (0.483 and 15.48), while the coefficients of both the independent variable are also higher. The same applies if we compare Eq.3 and Eq.4: a great difference in the values of $R^2$ and F (0.628 and 27.22 as opposed to 0.346 and 9.207) and, moreover, a coefficient of the lagged variable $IIND_{t-1}$ (Industrial Investment in the year t-1) which is significant only at the 0.05 level.

## The 'investment projects cycle'

We are aware, of course, of the extreme crudeness of the procedure adopted for discriminating between the two opposite hypotheses: nevertheless we do think that it provides sufficient indications in favour of the 'demand effect' approach. Whatever the case, if we accept the finding of a strong direct effect of investment on output, and recall the fact that it is the unplanned or, so to speak, the 'autonomous' part of investment that seems to be the relevant one, we may try to go somewhat deeper in the analysis of the investment cycle.

For the period 1965-1985 it is possible to trace the evolution of a variable which is very important from this point of view: this variable consists of the ratio of the value of the investment projects started in a particular year and the investment projects completed in the same year. This ratio constitutes a crucial indicator because it records, probably in a better way than the rate of growth of investment outlays, the variation in the degree of tension in the investment sphere: indeed, we may think of it as the heart-beat of an investment cycle, because it is exactly in the complex interplay of the mechanisms determining the numerator and denominator of this ratio that the 'regulation of the level of investment by negative feedback' appears [11].

In Fig. 2.7 we have plotted the values of this ratio, while in Fig. 2.8

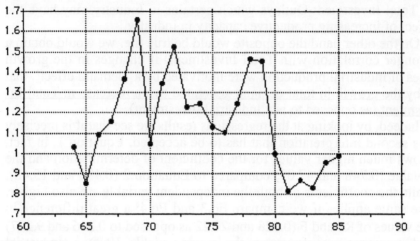

Figure 2.7    Ratio of total cost of started over completed investment projects

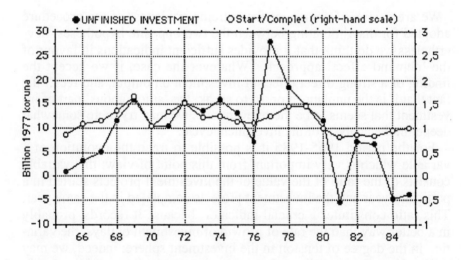

Figure 2.8  Starts/Completions ratio and Unfinished Investment

we have compared its evolution with the variations in unfinished investment, a second important variable to be scrutinised in order to analyse the cycle. First of all, there emerges a clear and definite cyclical character in the timing of the Starts/Completions variable, which follows almost strictly a five-year pattern. The increase in the value of this ratio, either because of an acceleration in the starting of new investment projects or because of a slowdown in the rate of completion of previous investment projects (with all the possible combinations, of course) begins at the start of the five-year planning period and continues until a peak is reached in the middle or final phase of the same period.

This increase has to be understood, indeed, as a signal of mounting pressures and shortages in the investment sector, with an ensuing increased disequilibrium that tends to spread to other sectors [Bauer 1978, pp. 250-255; Winiecki 1982, pp. 152-156]. In Fig. 2.8 it is important to note, moreover, that the increase in unfinished construction, a typical 'shortage' indicator, exhibits a similar time pattern.

After the peak of the cycle a slowdown phase, characterised by cuts or severe restraints in the starting of new projects, allows the restoring of a certain degree of equilibrium (or of a lower disequilibrium): in fact in the final years of every five-year planning period (1965,1970,1975,1980,1985) the value of the ratio is near or at the unit, which signals an exact balancing of new starts and completions.

It remains to be noted that in the last five-year period, 1981-85 the pattern of the cycle is completely reversed. This particular phenomenon has been caused by the strong and severe deflationary policy adopted by the authorities as a response to the high external disequilibrium and the deterioration in the balance of payments: this policy was implemented mainly through drastic cut backs in the approval of new investment projects. The value of the new starts has fallen dramatically from 110 to 70 billions koruna (about the level of 1971) from 1979 to 1981, recovering the 1979 level only on 1985.

Since this evolution has to be attributed almost entirely to an exogenous disturbance, the recession in 1979-1982, it cannot, in my opinion, be viewed as cyclical downswing, nor can we conclude, from the alterations in the pattern of the variables examined here in the period 1981-85, that there has been a serious modification in the underlying cyclical mechanism.

# Notes

REMARK: All statistical data originate from Czechoslovak statistical yearbooks (*Statistickà rocenka*, various issues) and from *Historickà statistickà rocenka*, 1985.

[1]  Gerritse, R. 'The Realm of Necessity: an Analysis of Industrial Business Cycles in Socialist Czechoslovakia', Ph.D. Thesis, University of Amsterdam, 1982, p.171

[2]  Goldmann, J. 'Fluctuations in the Growth Rate in a Socialist Economy and the Inventory Cycle', in: Bronfenbrenner, M. (ed.), *Is the Business Cycle Obsolete?*, Wiley & Sons, New York, 1969, pp.332-49

[3]  Gerritse, R., op.cit., pp.171-172

[4]  In the definition given by Gordon, for instance, a business cycle consists of 'recurring alternations of expansions and contractions in aggregate economic activity, the alternating movements in each direction being self-reinforcing and pervading virtually all parts of the economy' (cited in ICKES, B.W., 'Cyclical Fluctuations in Centrally Planned Economies: a Critique of the Literature', in *Soviet Studies*, vol. XXXVIII, n°1, Jan. 1986,p.51). That these alternation show also a periodicity is not strictly required.

[5]  Dahlstedt, R. *Cyclical Fluctuation under Central Planning: an Inquiry into the Nature and Causes of Cyclical Fluctuation in the Soviet Economy*, Acta Academiae Oeconomicae Helsingiensis, Series A:32, The Helsinki School of Economics, Helsinki 1980

[6]  Hutchings, R. 'Periodic Fluctuations in Soviet Industrial Growth Rates', *Soviet Studies*, vol. XX, n°3, 1969, pp.331-52.

[7]  Dahlstedt, R.,op.cit., p. 35

[8]  Dahlstedt, R.,op.cit., p. 36

[9]  Dahlstedt, R.,op.cit., pp. 110-115

[10] Gerritse, R., op.cit. pp.177-178.

[11] Bauer, T., 'Investment Cycles in Planned Economies', *Acta Oeconomica*, vol. 21 (3), 1978, p. 249

[12] Bauer, T.,op.cit., pp.250-255; Winiecki, J. 'Investment Cycles and Excess Demand Inflation in Planned Economies: Sources and Processes', *Acta Oeconomica*, vol.28 (1-2), 1982, pp.152-156.

# Bibliography

Bajt, A., (1971) 'Investment Cycles in European Socialist Economies: a Review Article', *Journal of Economic Literature*, vol. IX, n°1.

Bauer, T. (1986), 'From Cycles to Crisis? Recent Developments in East European Planned Economies and the Theory of Investment Cycles' a revised version of a paper presented at the Conference *Regulation, Cycles et Crises dans les Economies Socialistes*, Paris, EHESS, 13-14 march .

Bauer, T., (1978)'Investment Cycles in Planned Economies', *Acta Oeconomica*, vol. 21 (3), pp. 243-260.

Bauer, T.- Deak, A.- Soos, K.A., (1981), 'Investment Decision-Making in Hungary: Change and Continuity' in Bohnet,A.(ed.), *Gesamtwirtschaftliche Investitionssysteme: eine Vier-Länder-Studie, Duncker & Humblot, Berlin*, pp.163-72.

Bernasek, M., (1969), 'The Czechoslovak Economic Recession, 1962-65', *Soviet Studies*, vol. XX, n°4, April, pp.444-61

Boot, P., (1984), 'Industrial Cycles in the German Democratic Republic and Professor Wiles' Thesis', *The ACES Bulletin*, vol. XXVI, n°1, Spring, pp.1-26

Brada, J.C., (1981), 'The Czechoslovak Economic Recession, 1962-65: Comment', *Soviet Studies*, vol. XXII, n°3, pp. 402-5

Brody, A., (1983), 'About Investment Cycles and their Attenuation', *Acta Oeconomica*, vol. 31(1-2) pp. 37-51

Dahlstedt, R., (1980), *Cyclical Fluctuation under Central Planning: an Inquiry into the Nature and Causes of Cyclical Fluctuation in the Soviet Economy*, Acta Academiæ Oeconomicæ Helsingiensis, Series A:32, The Helsinki School of Economics, Helsinki.

Dedek, O., (1986), 'Investicni cyclus v socialistické ekonomice', Ekonomicky ústav CSAV, Prague.

Eysymontt, J.- Maciejewski, W., (1986), 'Socioeconomic Crises in Poland: a Model Approach', *Eastern European Economics*, vol. XXIV, n°3, Spring, pp. 6-23

Fallenbuchl, Z.M., (1985), 'Sources of Periodic Economic Crisis under the Centrally Planned Socialist Systems' in: Johnson,P.M.-Thompson, W.R. (eds.), *Rhythms in Politics and Economics*, New York, Praeger.

Gerritse, R., (1982), 'The Realm of Necessity: an Analysis of Industrial Business Cycles in Socialist Czechoslovakia', Ph.D. Thesis, University of Amsterdam.

Goldmann, J., (1964), 'Fluctuations and trend in the Rate of Economic Growth in Some Socialist Countries', *Economics of Planning*, n°2, pp.13-19

Goldmann, J., (1965), 'Short- and Long-Term Variations in the Growth-Rate and the Model of Functioning of a Socialist Economy', *Czechoslovak Economic Papers*, n°5, pp.35-46.

Goldmann, J., (1969), 'Fluctuations in the Growth Rate in a Socialist Economy and the Inventory Cycle', in: Bronfenbrenner, M. (ed.), *Is the Business Cycle Obsolete?*„ Wiley & Sons, New York, pp.332-49

Goldmann, J.- Flek, J., (1967), 'Vlnovity pohyb v tempu rustu a cyclus v dinamice zasob', *Planované hospodárství*, n°9.

Goldmann, J.- Kouba,K., (1969),*Economic Growth in Czechoslovakia: and Introduction to the Theory of Growth under Socialism*, Akademia, Prague.

Goldmann, J.- Kouba, K., (1984), 'Terms of Trade, Adjustment Processes, and the Economic Mechanism (A Quantitative Approach', *Acta Oeconomica*, vol. 32 (1-2), pp.137-60

Goldmann, J., (1976), 'The Czechoslovak Economy in the Seventies', *Eastern European Economics*, Spring, pp.3-35.

Grosfeld, I., (1986), 'Endogenous Planners and the Investment Cycle in Centrally Planned Economies', *Comparative Economic Studies*, Vol. XXVIII, n°1, pp.42-53.

Grosfeld,I., (1986), 'Endogenous Planners and the Investment Cycle in the Centrally Planned Economies', *Comparative Economic Studies*, vol.XXVIII, n°1, Spring, pp.42-53

Hutchings, R., (1969), 'Periodic Fluctuations in Soviet Industrial Growth Rates', *Soviet Studies*, vol. XX, n°3 pp.331-52

Ickes, B.W., (1986), 'Cyclical Fluctuations in Centrally Planned Economies: a Critique of the Literature', *Soviet Studies*, vol. XXXVIII, n°1, January, pp. 36-52

Kosta.J.- Levcik,F., (1985), 'Economic Crisis in the East European CMEA Countries', Research Project *Crises in Soviet-type Systems*, Study n°8, Wien.

Kyn, O.- Schrettl, W., (1979), W., *On the Stability of Contemporary Economic Systems*, Vandenhoeck & Ruprecht, Göttingen.

Kyn, O.- Schrettl, W.- Slama, J., (1979), 'Growth Cycles in Centrally Planned Economies. An Empirical Test', Kyn, O.- Schrettl, W. (eds.), *On the Stability of Contemporary Economic Systems*, Vandenhoeck & Ruprecht, Göttingen, pp. 109-132

Lacko, M., (1980), 'Cumulating and Easing of Tensions (a Simple Model of the Cyclical Development of Investments in Hungary', *Acta Oeconomica*, vol. 24(3-4), pp.357-77

Olivera, J., (1960), 'Cyclical Economic Growth under Collectivism', *Kyklos*, n°2, pp.229-255.

Roland, G., (1987), 'Investment Growth Fluctuations in the Soviet Union: an Econometric Analysis', *Journal of Comparative Economics*, vol. 11, n°2, June, pp.192-206.

Sapir, J., (1985), 'Conflit sociaux et fluctuations économiques en URSS: l'exemple de le période 1950-1965', *Annales ESC*, n° 4, pp.737-779

Soos, K.A., (1976), 'Causes of Investment Fluctuations in the Hungarian Economy', *Eastern European Economics*, Winter 1975-76, pp.25-36

Soos, K.A., (1978), 'Some General Problems of the Hungarian Investment System', *Acta Oeconomica*, vol. 21(3), pp.223-242

Staller, G.J., (1964), 'Fluctuations in Economic Activity: Planned and Free Market Economies, 1950-1960', American Economic Review, June.

Wiles, P., (1982), 'Are there Communist Economic Cycles ?', *The ACES Bulletin*, vol. XXIV, n°2, Summer, pp. 1-19

Winiecki, J., (1982), 'Investment Cycles and Excess Demand Inflation in Planned Economies: Sources and Processes', *Acta Oeconomica*, vol.28 (1-2), pp.147-160.

# 3 Economic fluctuations in China

GIANNI SALVINI

## Introduction

In order to analyse Chinese economic cycles, it is useful to compare them with the theory of cycles in centrally planned economies (CPE's). T. Bauer (1978) explains why in CPE's we can observe relatively regular investment cycles. The main source of investment cycles is overinvestment; given that the planning system in CPE's has never meant full centralization of decision making, but a peculiar distribution of this between different levels of the management hierarchy, overinvestment arises from the following circumstances:

1) Plan fulfilment is the main indicator used in the evaluation of the performance of managers. Obtaining more investment makes plan fulfilment easier. Enterprise managers are, therefore, interested in obtaining as much investment as possible.

2) The inability of the centre to control the investment claims.

3) Increasing the rate of accumulation and extension of investment is given a high priority by central planners, in order to raise the political prestige of the power elite. Increasing the rate of growth and the rate of accumulation becomes an end in itself, while the standard of living is only a constraint to the former.

Overinvestment emerges as the investment projects approved in the five-year plans involve investment outlays which exceed to a large extent the amount calculated when the plan was elaborated and when national balances were drawn up.

This is the way in which relatively regular investment cycles take place, particularly four-phase investment cycles.

— Run-up: many new investment projects are started at the same time. This leads to the rapid extension in the stock of investment projects in progress; but if this is compensated partly by the completion of a relatively high number of the projects which were started earlier, only a moderate increase in investment outlays will be observed. The process does not lead to tensions.

— Rush: starting new investment projects is continued, and the projects started in the first phase require higher investment outlays. The increase in total investment outlays becomes faster and exceeds the initially planned growth rate. The shortage of investment goods and services re-emerges or is sharpened, and the rate of investment and of accumulation in national income rises. Either the growth of consumption will be delayed or the balance of trade worsened.

— Halt: a smaller number of new investment projects are approved, but the continuation of investment projects started earlier is promoted, as the planners intend to work off the investment engagement through forcing a rapid growth of investment outlays and of construction output even at the sacrifice of a shift between the uses of national income. The beginning of this phase marks the upper turning point in the cycle.

— Slowdown: in order to alleviate the tension in the utilisation of national income the central planners ultimately curb the growth of investment outlays, and the approval coefficient continues to fall. Less important investment projects in progress are delayed or suspended, so that priority projects may be accelerated. Due to this more projects will be completed. As a result of the slowdown, the shortage of investment goods is alleviated, the rate of investment falls and the situation improves with respect to those uses of national income which were suppressed earlier.

Meanwhile, due to the more balanced situation in the economy, the selection of investment projects is less severe, the approval coefficient rises again and a new cycle begins with the run-up. This marks the lower turning point in the cycle.

Overstrained investment accompanied by cyclical fluctuations has two main unfavourable effects on economic growth.

First, the fact that more investment projects are simultaneously in progress than enabled by the investment potential of the economy results in prolongation of construction periods and delays in completion. The most important consequence is that a higher share of accumulation funds than necessary is tied up in the stock of unfinished investment and therefore one per cent of growth of fixed capital requires more accumulation than otherwise.

Apart from this, the confusion and delays of different kinds mean that output is reduced compared with the additional inputs required. These effects increase the necessary investment outlays per one per cent of growth of additional income, i.e. they result in a lower growth rate in the long run.

Secondly, the prolonged completion of investment projects is unfavourable for technological development, since the new capacity may embody the technology available at the time of projection and the possibilities for the adoption of new trends in technological development through quick realization of new investment projects are insufficient.

In the Chinese case, the three circumstances which cause overinvestment to arise have always been in existence; however, investment cycles in China have not followed strictly the four-phase scheme and have not been regular. In fact, Chinese investment cycles have been highly correlated with overall economic fluctuations, at least until the late 1960's. These fluctuations were determined by political shifts and agricultural fluctuations rather than by regular economic cycles.

The unfavourable effects of overinvestment on economic growth are, however, clearly present.

### Overinvestment and investment efficiency in China's economic development

Persistent overinvestment in the Chinese economy can be tested by looking at the efficiency of investment in the long run.

The decreasing efficiency of investment is shown in Table 3.1 (Ishikawa, 1984). Despite the steady increase in the rate of domestic investment, the marginal output-domestic investment ratio systematically declined, particularly during the 1970's.

The consequence was that the average annual rate of growth of national income did not show any increasing trend. On the other hand, the marginal output-state capital construction investment ratio also declined systematically side by side with the decline in the marginal output-domestic investment ratio. Columns [4] and [5] indicate that this was caused both by the decline in the rate of fixed capital assets formation and by the decline in the marginal output-fixed capital assets ratio.

Data reported by Maruyama (1982) show that this pattern of declining efficiency can be explained by the following vicious circle (see Ta-

Table 3.1
Rate of domestic investment and marginal output-investment ratio
of the economy
(five-year plan periods)

| | Rate of domestic investment | Annual growth rate of national income | Marginal output-investment ratio | Marginal output-capital construction investment ratio | Rate of fixed capital asset formation | Marginal output-fixed capital assets ratio |
|---|---|---|---|---|---|---|
| 1 FYP (1953-57) | 0.242 | 8.9 | 0.350 | 0.595 | 0.834 | 0.717 |
| 2 FYP (1958-62) | 0.308 | −3.1 | 0.010 | 0.014 | 0.714 | 0.020 |
| Adjustment period (1963-65) | 0.227 | 14.5 | 0.570 | 1.087 | 0.871 | 1.248 |
| 3 FYP (1966-70) | 0.263 | 8.4 | 0.260 | 0.431 | 0.595 | 0.724 |
| 4 FYP (1971-75) | 0.330 | 5.6 | 0.160 | 0.266 | 0.614 | 0.433 |
| 1976-79 | 0.334 | 6.1 | 0.208 | — | — | 0.340 |

Source: Ishikawa (1984).

bles 3.2 and 3.3):

High growth targets » high rate of investment » excessive investment in capital construction » disorder in the supply of materials and greater imbalance between industries » soaring prices of materials and construction delays.

In CPE's, it has been observed that this kind of vicious circle leads to a curb in investment with consequent slowdown of the whole economic activity; investment then rises again when imbalances have been corrected.

In other words, investment cycles determine economic cycles.

In the Chinese case, overinvestment affected economic cycles especially from the late 1960s onwards, although it did play some role in preceding years (for example in 1957). In the first two decades of socialist development, however, agricultural fluctuations and political shifts played the major role in determining economic and investment cycles.

Table 3.2

Rise in construction investment costs

| | Coal pit construction (450,000 tons annual production) | | Large and medium-size cement plants (annual production of 200,000 tons or more) | | Construction of trunk railway lines (per 100 km) | | Rate of completion of large and medium-size projects during year in question (%) | Ratio of investment expended for uncompleted construction in the total amount of investment allocated for year in question (%) |
|---|---|---|---|---|---|---|---|---|
| | Average construction period (months) | Investment per unit of capacity (Yuan/Ton) | Average construction period (months) | Investment per unit of capacity (Yuan/ton) | Average construction period (months) | Amount of investment (1,000 Yuan) | | |
| 1st five-year plan period | 30 | 37 | 28 | 74 | 11.7 | 573 | 15.5 | 62.9 |
| 2nd five-year plan period | 25 | 28.1 | 36 | 97 | 14.8 | 461 | 8.1 | |
| 3rd five-year plan period | | | | | 16.7 | 1,734 | 11.5 | 175.4 |
| 4th five-year plan period | 52 | 41.9 | 73 | 121 | 21.5 | 1,414 | 9.4 | 165.7 |
| 1976 – 79 | 69.6 | 62.7 | 90 | 114 | 28.8 | 2,474 | 7.4 | 210 (1976) 213 (1977) |

Source: Maruyama (1982).

Table 3.3
Rise in cost of croducts of major iron and steel
and nonferrous metal enterprises
(Yuan/ton)

| Item | 1966 | 1978 | 1980 | Rate of increase 1980/1966 (%) |
|---|---|---|---|---|
| Iron ore | 5.48 | 6.12 | 6.84 | 25 |
| Coke | 63.02 | 66.03 | 81.20 | 29 |
| Pig iron | 105 | 138 | 161.44 | 54 |
| Converter steel ingots | 228 | 231 | 253.90 | 11.3 |
| Hot-rolled sheet metal | 260 | 408 | 455.51 | 75.2 |
| Welded steel pipes | 408 | 521 | 524.27 | 28.5 |
| Refined copper | 2,088 | 2,489 | 2,687.66 | 28.7 |
| Lead | 931 | 900 | 1,058.37 | 13.7 |
| Zinc | 1,399 | 1,441 | 1,403.12 | 0.3 |
| Alumina | 218 | 199 | 206.50 | −5.3 |
| Tungsten | 4,378 | 5,190 | 5,974.75 | 36.5 |
| Molybdenum | 7,822 | 8,285 | 9,253.92 | 18.3 |
| No. 2 purple sheet copper | 6,460 | 6,428 | 6,106.73 | −5.5 |
| Industrial pure aluminum sheet | 2,737 | 3,792 | 3,633.70 | 32.8 |
| Average for 16 iron and steel products | | | | 33.2 |
| Average for 18 nonferrous metal products | | | | 46.4 |

Source: Maruyama (1982).

## Investment cycles in China

From 1952 onwards, six investment cycles can be observed: 1953-57, 1958-62, 1963-68, 1969-76, 1977-81 and 1982.

### 1953-57

In 1952, agriculture's NMP accounted for 57% of total NMP, compared to 19% for industry; in 1957, shares were 46% for agriculture and 28% for industry.

Hence, the high rates of growth of NMP in 1953 and 1956 were the outcome of good harvests in 1952-53 and 1955, while the lowering of NMP rates of growth in 1954 and 1955 were induced by the lower growth of agriculture in 1954.

Besides, Cheng (1982) shows that between 1952 and 1960 changes in agricultural output, particularly grain output, invariably induced an investment cycle with roughly a one-year lag. This explains the investment boom in 1956 (+ 52%).

Despite the good performance of agriculture in 1956 (+ 5.3%), in 1957 the trough of the first cycle occurred. Investment dropped in absolute terms (− 6%), because of the first overinvestment crisis. In fact, in 1956 the rate of unfinished capacity reached 24.6%.

### 1958-62

In 1957, it was believed that it would take at least two or three years for the country to pass through the phase of slowdown to reach equilibrium, but the economy jumped into the Great Leap Forward. Here, we can stress how moderate growth of agriculture in 1958 caused a spectacular but unsustainable jump in industrial production and in investment in 1958-59. A rapid decline followed in 1961 and 1962. The rate of unfinished capacity reached 31.2% in 1960, but in this cycle the overinvestment crisis was only part of the overall economic crisis, caused by the strong emphasis that was placed on political objectives and also by planning mistakes.

### 1963-68

The peak of 1964 was reached after the recovery of agriculture, brought about by the new farm policy, combining changes in the commune system and in peasant incentives with a greater supply of inputs to agriculture (farm machinery and chemical fertilizers).

The sharp rates of growth of investment in 1963 and 1964 were a reaction to the steep decline in 1961 and 1962, so the total amount of investment in 1963 and 1964 was relatively small. In fact, in 1965 the rate of unfinished capacity was only 6.4%. In the same year, investment grew by 30.7%, and in 1966 the rate of unfinished capacity reached 29.6%.

This means that the economy was entering a run-up phase, with soaring overinvestment.

Again; political factors (the Cultural Revolution) disrupted the investment cycle. Hence, we find the trough of investment in 1967 and 1968. In those years, despite the reduction of investment and due to the Cultural Revolution, the rate of unfinished capacity remained at abnormally high levels (49.4% in 1967 and 54.1% in 1968).

*1969-76*

In this cycle, the relationship between fluctuations in agriculture, NMP and investment was less clear than in past cycles. In 1971, for the first time industry's share of NMP was greater than that of agriculture (42% against 39%).

Nevertheless, the leadership adopted the economic policy of a 'New Leap Forward' after an abundant harvest, in 1970-71. But the peak of investment in 1975 (+ 17.6%) was not determined by agricultural growth in the preceding year (+ 4.4%).

In 1976 NMP fell by 3%, industry NMP by 5.7%, investment by 3.9% and agriculture NMP grew by 1.1%.

The trough of this cycle was also caused by political factors, but several authors label it an 'economy of shortage' crisis, due to overinvestment and to the declining efficiency in the use of resources from the late 1960's on. Here are some of the causes:

1. In the 1970s, the policy of 'walking on two legs' regained momentum, leading to a rapid expansion of smaller-scale industries in the provinces (the number of industrial enterprises grew from 195,000 in 1970 to 294,000 in 1976). According to Ishikawa (1983), this expansion was accompanied by a large financial deficit;

2. The weakening of planning gave more autonomy to local governments in determining their plans for basic construction, with the consequent expansion of these beyond the country's capacity and the rise in the rate of uncompleted capacity (the annual average rate for 1969-76 was 39%, compared to 29% for 1963-68);

3. At the same time, the financial autonomy of enterprises was reduced with the abolishment, in 1967, of the enterprise bonus fund

(retention by the enterprise of a fixed portion of profits) allowed to state owned enterprises in the 1950's. Instead, the authorities launched the scheme of labor welfare funds, which was set up on a consolidated basis as a percentage of the total wages of the enterprise concerned. This reduction of financial autonomy probably encouraged carelessness in the use of funds.

4. In the period up to 1966, the depreciation funds in state enterprises had to be remitted to the state. The state then handed them back to the enterprises under a comprehensive scheme. The replacement and rebuilding allowances were all supplied from the state budget. In the period 1966-75, the basic depreciation allowance was retained by the enterprise and this often meant that the allowance was used for basic construction.

5. Since the second half of the 1970s, excessive increase in inventories has been a major factor in the decline of efficiency. There was no interest cost for the storage of unused materials. The unused and unsalable equipment and materials were not counted as inventory costs for the enterprise concerned but were, in effect, an implicit cost to the state. Under these circumstances, the best policy for the production units to adopt was to make every effort to apply for more funds and more materials for basic construction, because they helped create more room for expansion and there was less risk of having insufficients funds.

*1977-81*

In 1977 a new short cycle began, with its peak in 1978 and its trough in 1981. According to Maruyama, the inauguration in 1978 of the ambitious Ten Year Plan occurred when the economy still needed to enter into a slowdown stage. Total fixed investment in that year rose by 22%, total NMP by 13.8% and NMP of industry by 17.8%.

The rate of unfinished capacity, although much lower than in the mid-1970's, was 25.7% in 1978, about at the same level as 1956, the year before the first overinvestment crisis. Probably, behind the 1978 decision there was a lack of understanding of the law of investment cycles and an exaggerated tendency to attribute past growth fluctuations to political factors, particularly to ultra-leftism.

The economic readjustment policy was adopted in April 1979 but, in 1979 and 1980, investment continued to grow, although at moderate rates (4.6% and 6.7% respectively). The failure to reduce investment can be attributed to two reasons:

a) the central government's own investment fever, related to the introduction of foreign technology (in 1979, delays in the implementation of these large-scale projects accounted for 76% of uncompleted investment);

b) the new non-budgetary investment fever, due to the expansion of the right of self-management of local finances.

The slowdown came at last in 1981, with a 10.5% reduction in total fixed investment and slow growth in industry (1.2%). The investment cut was achieved by postponing or cancelling some imports of large-scale complete plants and by imposing restrictions on the investment and funds held by local governments and enterprises.

However, the slowdown in industry (particularly heavy industry) threatened the policy of giving priority to light industry, because the supply of raw and construction materials and equipments became insufficient. Besides, the slack performance of heavy industry adversely affected national revenues (revenues from heavy industry account for 60% of total revenues taken in taxes and profits from all industry).

Hence, in the latter half of 1981 and at the beginning of 1982, heavy industry was revitalised and investment started to grow again in 1982 (+ 26.6%) and in the following years.

## The economic reforms and the non budgetary investment fever

The first step of the reforms was the introduction of a profit-sharing system on a trial basis in 1979 and on a broader basis in 1981 (80% of state owned enterprises), with the 'economic responsibility system'. Under this system, enterprises negotiated for annual profit remittance quotas with their supervisory agencies.

Despite these incentives, there was little evidence of improved efficiency in state owned enterprises. R.M. Field estimated that output per 100 yuan of fixed assets declined by 14.5% from 1978 to 1982. Continued inefficiency was due to the 'expansion' and 'quantity' drives, allowed by the overdecentralisation of financial resources which maintained the soft budget constraint.

This situation was the outcome of the following problems related to the reform process:

1) Despite the stress on the need to use resources in a more efficient way, relatively few non-economic enterprises were shut down. The ones closed were mainly small-scale and local enterprises, not large scale and state-owned ones.

2) Retention of profits increased sharply, reaching 85% of increased profits in 1983, while the underfulfilment of the profit target was rarely punished.

3) Prices and taxes became in a certain sense negotiable. With the partial liberalisation of trade outside state channels, gaps were formed between plan and market prices; local officials allowed enterprises to negotiate the proportion of output they sold at each price, providing disguised subsidies for loss-making factories.

The same happened to taxes, with local officials offering tax exemptions or reductions. These were important factors for enterprise profitability.

4) Bank loans were granted on such soft terms, that the burden actually born by enterprises was quite small.

Hence, extra-budgetary investment grew from 27.7% of total investment in fixed assets in 1978 to 59.3% in 1982 (Table 3.4).

Table 3.4
Sources of investment in fixed assets, 1978-1985
(billions Yuan)*

|      | Total  | Budgetary    | Extra-budgetary |
|------|--------|--------------|-----------------|
| 1978 | 66.87  | 48.35 (72.3) | 18.52 (27.7)    |
| 1979 | 69.94  | 55.07 (78.7) | 14.87 (21.3)    |
| 1980 | 74.59  | 45.97 (61.6) | 28.62 (38.4)    |
| 1981 | 66.75  | 36.33 (54.4) | 30.42 (45.6)    |
| 1982 | 84.53  | 34.37 (40.7) | 50.16 (59.3)    |
| 1983 | 95.20  | 42.22 (44.3) | 52.98 (55.7)    |
| 1984 | 118.52 | (41.2)       | (58.8)          |
| 1985 | 168.15 | (29.2)       | (70.8)          |

* Figures in parentheses represent percent of total investment
Source: Statistical Yearbook of China

In 1983-84, new measures were introduced to control the use of resources, beginning with the introduction of a 10% tax on extra-budgetary funds on the 1st of January, 1983; the tax was raised to 15% in mid-year.

The second measure was the introduction of 'substituting taxes for profits': all large and medium sizes state enterprises were due to shift from the system of remitting profits to paying taxes on profits, with enterprises being given greater autonomy in disposing of the residual income. With the completion of this measure, profit remittance will be completely replaced by a series of taxes designed to tax away all benefits accruing to factors external to the enterprise, so that enterprises are rewarded only for profits due to their performance. The present industrial-commercial (turnover) tax will be broken down into four parts: the product tax, the value added tax, business tax and salt tax, which will tax away differential profitability across products. This system will exclude small state-owned enterprises with fixed assets under 1.5 million yuan and annual profits of 200,000 yuan or less; these enterprises will be contracted or leased to collectives or individuals over a three years period, with the contractors responsible for paying capital charges and income taxes on profits. This program will affect approximately half of the 81.000 state enterprises presently classified as 'small scale'. The rationale for the tax-for-profit scheme is to formalise the financial relationship between the state and enterprises and reduce the negotiability of profit remittance.

Despite these measures, in 1984 domestic loans and self-generated funds still accounted for 58.8% of total investment in fixed assets (EIU) and investment in capital construction grew by 43% in 1985, while it seems that investment rate of growth began to decline in 1986 (in the first nine months of 1986 investment in fixed assets grew by 18.7% against 33.7% in the same period of 1985). Anyway, the most pressing problems identified by government spokesmen during 1986 remained inefficient use of resources, continued and acute shortages of inputs to industry and excessive investment demand.

## Conclusions

As stated by Kornai, '... the explanation of chronic shortage, of suction, and of the functioning of a resource-constrained system is to be found not in the financial sphere, or in special features of price information, but at a deeper level, in institutional relationships and in behavioral regularities which the institutional relations foster in decision-makers'. So, the problem facing Chinese reformers is how to find a workable combination of economic incentives and administrative controls. Throughout the first phase of reform, local governments saw decentralising reforms as a way to further extend their control over resources; in the second period, however, the reforms are aimed at reversing the trend of growing local influence over industrial production which has characterized the past two decades.

However, according to the latest information, the effort towards control has not brought about the expected results; but if slowdown and equilibrium cannot be reached, the readjustment of the industrial structure and the implementation of a new, more balanced, economic growth will become impossible tasks.


## Notes

I wish to acknowledge the advice and assistance of Roberto Maganza.


## References

Bauer, T. (1978), 'Investment Cycles in Planned Economies', *Acta Œconomica*, vol. 21, pp. 243-260.

Cheng Chu-Yuan (1982), *China's Economic Development; Growth and Structural Change*, Boulder, Westview Press.

Field, R.M. (1984), 'Political Conflict and Industrial Growth in China',*China Quarterly*, December, pp. 9-55.

Ishikawa, S. (1984), 'China Economic Growth since 1949: An Assessment', *China Quarterly*, December, pp. 96-102.

Kornai, J. (1980), *Economic of Shortage*, New York, North-Holland.

Maruyama, N. (1982), 'The Mechanism of the Industrial Development in China', *The Developing Economies*.

Maruyama, N. (1984), 'The Investment Cycle in China: Why Overexpansion of Investment Persist', *China Newsletter*, n. 45.

Shimakura, T. (1982), 'Cycles in the Chinese Economy and their Politico-Economic Implications', *The Developing Economies*.

# 4 Regular investment cycles or irregular investment fluctuations under central planning?

KAROLY ATTILA SOOS

The idea of cyclical fluctuations under central planning has been seriously challenged in the literature. Are there regular fluctuations in European socialist economies (ESE's)? By just looking at any relevant non-Hungarian time series anybody can give a negative answer to this question. However, this fact does not mean at all that the findings of the research of cycles in ESE's are useless. This research has managed to describe all the important elements of a theory of cyclical fluctuations under central planning. Yet the rub is that these elements do not work always with equal strength in all ESE's, and exogenous factors randomise their functioning. Nevertheless, the 'elements' in question are not pure fiction. On the contrary, they are rooted in the reality of ESE's, and on this basis they have both analytical and predictive values.

Innumerable text-books published in East European socialist countries have repeated the thesis that there are not and cannot be cyclical fluctuations in socialist economies [1]. Although these publications — together with similarly oriented articles, etc. — represent the overwhelming majority of the literature of the topic, research workers interested in socialist economic cycles have not paid much attention to them, because they have been based on prejudices, rather than research.

Yet dogmatic declarations are not the only denials of the existence of socialist economic cycles. Such views — in this case we have to say: conclusions — are also expressed in some works based on profound research. The articles of Pèter Mihàlyi (1986) and Peter Wiles (1982) belong to the latter category. These articles, like other publications of both authors, fully merit our attention. All who are interested in the topic should reflect on their arguments. I myself have learned much from them , but I still disagree with them on some basic points.

Fortunately the two articles complement each other. Mihàlyi makes use of sophisticated methods of mathematical statistics in analysing ESE's time series and arrives at the conclusion that

> 'various real shocks hitting the East European economies at random seem to generate so big fluctuations that the impact of internal cyclical forces, in terms of time regularity, is discernible, if at all, only to a very limited extent'.

I think, *if at all*, is here an exaggeration. Wiles also underlines the lack of periodical regularity in Eastern European economic fluctuations, because of which, according to him, 'there are no cycles proprement dit'. Yet his article has a theoretical approach and contains analyses of the concrete causes of many individual peaks and troughs in the economic (mainly investment) growth in various (not only European) socialist countries.

As he states:

> 'Moods of unrealistic optimism and pessimism could shake the Politburo at moments of rising and falling (or accelerating and decelerating) investment, thus generating excessive and unmaintainable peaks, followed by unnecessary troughs; and indeed some students of the subject have suggested that this is what does happen'.

But

> 'The trouble is that the crucial optimistic seizures, which must begin the cycle, are not generated by economic phenomena'.

These peaks are political according to the author, though in most cases they are followed by 'basically economic' troughs. The decisions which bring about the peaks are political; the author also stresses this by calling their author the Politburo, and not the *central planner* , although the latter in traditional analytic parlance obviously includes the former. But in these situations — when fast investment growth has let

62

to serious disequilibria in the economy — the following trough is already *basically economic*:

> 'the Politburo, not out of any ideological compulsion, reacts simply as a good manager, plucks up its courage, defies the satraps and curtails investment starts'

Still, Wiles also finds exceptions to these rules: political troughs which are not enforced by economic disturbances, and two kinds of *basically economic* peaks — (a) those (Hungarian) ones which are politically ordered, but on an economic basis (on the basis of the previous strong improvement of the foreign trade balance); and (b) those which are not even ordered by the Politburo.

In discussing these theses I shall follow my own logic, and speak mainly about the fluctuations of the 1960s and 1970s, in some cases of the 1950s and only in the final stages of the 1980s. I begin with the latter (b): do investment accelerations actually occur without the central planners' decision?

# 1. The scope of central control over macrodynamic processes

According to Wiles, yes, in two cases: in 1959 in Czechoslovakia, and in 1967 in Hungary. Both peaks are consequences of model changes, namely wide-range investment decentralisations. Yet if we turn to the details (as they are described by the author), the explanation becomes so different for the two cases that its validity is strongly doubtful.

## 1.1. Investment booms are always caused by expansionist policies

As Wiles writes, in Czechoslovakia the 1958 investment decentralisation led to many new project-starts and high investment outlays in 1959. Whereas in Hungary exactly the opposite occurred: decentralisation took place after acceleration, during the trough of 1968. In 1967, enterprises were striving to exploit the last gratuitous investment financing possibilities; this would be the explanation for the acceleration of that year.

Of course, enterprises were striving to do so. But in my opinion that was rather the excuse of the central planners than the actual reason for the investment boom. Wiles also remarks that both this peak and the subsequent trough:

'also partake of the normal reaction (of the Hungarian central planners — K.A.S.) to the previous year's balance of payments'.

With regard to the investment peak of 1959 in Czechoslovakia, it was (as described by Bauer 1981, pp. 86-92) part of the general 'Great Leap Forward' atmosphere in Eastern Europe at the time (and thus, of course, brought about by the central planners). The latter explanation is accepted by Wiles for the 1959 peaks in some other countries: the GDR, Bulgaria, Romany, and Poland. Let me point out that this 'leap' coincided with wide-range investment decentralisation not only in Czechoslovakia, but also in Poland. If we look at the figures (cf. Podolski 1973, p. 230 and 235) we can see that the enormous growth of decentralised investments caused the 1959 investment boom (apart from Czechoslovakia) in Poland, too. And if we listen to the planners who were searching for excuses, we may think that it was a 'spontaneous' process.

But if we reflect on the problem more profoundly, we have to conclude that central planners may decentralise investments in an optimistic mood, with a loose regulation of the global volume of decentralised investments, bringing about (of course, with the help of the firms' always intensive 'investment hunger') an investment boom (as happened in Czechoslovakia and Poland in 1959); and they may decentralise in a pessimistic mood, with a strict regulation of the global volume of decentralised investments, bringing about an investment trough (as happened in Hungary in 1968). In other words, model changes do not cause investment booms.

On the contrary, what Wiles finds (only) typical seems to be an absolute rule: I myself have never heard about an investment boom in any socialist country which was brought about by anything other than expansionist economic policies.

## 1.2. Investment troughs with and without nearly convertible national currency

If fast investment growth is always caused by expansionist policies, does this mean that expansionist policies always cause fast investment growth?

No, because sources for fast growth may not be available. But here the origin of the sources is of crucial importance. The sources may be *(i)* increased domestic production and/or *(ii)* diminished exports and/or increased imports of investment goods.

*(i)*, of course, may often not be available [2]. And more important from our point of view, central planners may err in their estimates of its availability. They may erroneously think that it is disposable. A similar mistake in the case of *(ii)* until 1981 was practically impossible, simply because that source was always available. With regard to the crucial import side, both the supply of goods and the financing possibilities (i.e. the credit supply) for imports from socialist countries have, of course, been limited. But for imports from western markets, jolts in the supply of goods were sporadic (except perhaps in 1969 and 1974), and in the credit supply (until 1981) nonexistent (borrowing could always be increased).

Does this mean that the acceleration of investment growth was always possible for all ESE's at the expense of the foreign trade balance?

No, not for all ESE's. If investment is about one-third of the produced national income (PNI), and export about one-twentieth of the latter (to take the case of the Soviet Union), then obviously any significant acceleration of investment growth at the expense of the foreign trade balance would necessarily entail an absurdly increasing debt/export ratio. In the Hungarian and the Bulgarian cases the export/PNI ratio is not one twentieth but about one-third or one half. This difference is enormous and means that in the latter countries investment acceleration at the expense of the foreign trade balance does not necessarily entail an absurdly increasing debt/export ratio.

Consequently, investment acceleration at the expense of the foreign trade balance was until 1981 always possible for Bulgaria and Hungary. Several other ESE's, Czechoslovakia, the GDR, Poland, and Romania, fall between these extreme cases [3], as does Yugoslavia with its relatively modest visible export performance but large amounts of invisible exports [4].

For the latter *transitional* group of countries, I have no ready answer to the question as to whether investment acceleration at the expense of the foreign trade balance does or does not necessarily lead to an absurdly increasing debt/export ratio. However, fortunately, it is not my, but the central planners' answer which is important here. The question faced by the planners when they are eager to have fast investment growth is: are they ready to accept a serious deterioration in the foreign trade balance as a price of this growth?

The answer of Soviet planners has, of course, always been negative. But no other country's case is so simple!

The least complicated seem to be the Hungarian and Yugoslav cases. In Hungarian economic plans, ambitious planned investment growth was often, e.g. in 1970, 1974, coupled with a deliberate deterioration of the foreign trade balance (not only with socialist, but also with non socialist countries). In other years, e.g. in 1977, not only investment acceleration, but also the maintenance of the previous year's foreign trade balance was prescribed [5]. That was, of course, a *contradictio in adiecto* in the Hungarian circumstances of high import intensity of investment outlays. But the contradiction in question did not really appear in practical economic policy. That is to say, in 1977 investment acceleration remained a 'valid', and the maintenance of the foreign trade balance became an 'invalid' objective: investment growth was 14.4 per cent (after –0.3 per cent in the previous year) and the deficit in non-rouble foreign trade was 28.4 billion forints (exceeding the deficit of the previous year by 4.9 billion).

In other words, planned foreign trade processes, and actual foreign trade processes to an even greater extent, followed the investment policies, if the latter were expansionist. Such developments are not surprising in a country in which the capacities of production of investment goods cannot keep pace with the periodic accelerated growth of investment demand, and where the national currency is convertible. The first of these conditions holds for Hungary: whereas the second condition, as everybody knows, does not hold. The Hungarian forint is not convertible. Yet those who know the functioning of the Hungarian economic mechanism before the liquidity difficulties of 1981 will not be really surprised if I say that then the Hungarian forint was nearly convertible. It may be objected that the Hungarian economy was even then an economy of shortage: *ipso facto* the currency had to be far from actual convertibility. But far and near are relative terms. In the first half of the 1960s a very important change occurred in this respect: it became much easier for the enterprises which had forints to get dollars. A less important but even more radical change occurred in the availability of roubles: their supply for Hungarian enterprises became unlimited. This was not the case for the enterprises of most other socialist countries.

Of course, when increasing foreign trade deficits led to austerity in investment policies, then not only the growth of investment demand was cut back, but also the 'degree of convertibility' of the national currency diminished. But it again implies that in expansionist periods the 'degree' in question increased. Under these conditions investment expenditure always followed investment demand. And, because the latter was regulated by central planners' policies (by subsequent waves of expansionist and austerity policies), we can state: the speed of investment growth was under central control. Central planners' decisions and only central planners' decisions led to both accelerations and decelerations of investment growth.

Everything stated so far also holds for Yugoslavia. Analysts of Yugoslav macroeconomic processes also underline the dependence in the developments of the foreign trade balance on the fluctuations of domestic demand (cf. e.g. Horvat 1971, Bajt 1972, Kovac 1973), which is a sign of a nearly convertible national currency. Ambitious investment plans were, as in Hungary, often coupled with planned deteriorations of the foreign trade balance, e.g. in 1974 [6]. Whenever these plan figures nevertheless contradicted each other, one of them proved to be mere wishful thinking, not followed by actual policies. For example, in the expansionist atmosphere of the elaboration of the annual plan (socio-economic policy resolution) for 1970, nobody could seriously think that the foreseen fast growth of exports and the improvement of the foreign trade balance [7] would actually be implemented. Of course direct testing of the central planners' thinking is not possible, but anyway, they did not do anything to encourage the implementation of the latter objective, and the acceleration of economic (including investment) growth (investment expenditure increased by 15.0 per cent, after 8.4 and 7.1 percent in the two previous years) led to an increase in the foreign trade deficit (from 659 to 1194 million dollars).

'Nearly convertible national currency', the concept upon which the preceding analysis is built, is of course connected with market-type decentralisation introduced in both the Yugoslav and the Hungarian economies. I must ,say that the connection in question does not seem to be a very close, direct one. The quasi-convertibility in question appeared in Hungary some years before the introduction of the New Economic Mechanism (1968), and in Yugoslavia about the mid-fifties, that is after the first economic reforms, but long before the radical reforms of the 1960s. On this basis I think that a certain kind of 'quasi-convertibility' may exist even in the framework of a traditional, highly centralised planned economy. Central planners may find that coupling fast increase of (investment) demand with severe restrictions of imports and forced growth of exports could bring about, rather than an 'efficient mobilisation of domestic production capacities', serious economic disturbances. Thus they may open import channels for satisfying investment needs which are created by their own investment decisions. If, as it is usual under traditional central planning, in the domestic distribution of investment goods the role of money is rather passive, being substituted for by wide-spread administrative allocation, then the opening in question means a quasi-convertibility of the administrative assignments rather than that of money. In other words, the investor may get an import licence for a certain machine not because he has the money to pay the price, but because his investment is included into the national economic plan (and, of course, because the machine cannot be produced in the country). The Hungarian reality in the years preceding the introduction of the reform was similar to this kind of quasi-convertibility.

Yet that was a very exceptional and typically transitional phenomenon. We are faced here with a behaviour specific to the central planners. They always open import channels when they begin to stimulate investment growth, and they always cut back the growth of investment demand when they begin to cut back imports and to stimulate exports. Such planners attribute a relatively (I will come back to this 'relatively' in my conclusion) high importance to the internal equilibrium of the national economy. At the same time, they have to recognise the great importance of foreign trade (including that of Western foreign trade) for the functioning of the national economy. Such planners probably have to be reform-minded and to introduce an economic reform, as Hungarian planners did in 1968. So we return to the above statement: nearly convertible national currency is connected with market-type decentralisation.

Thus it is not surprising that the national currencies of other ESE's, which did not introduce similar reforms, were not (even) nearly convertible. (Czechoslovakia, with its political disruptions in the 1960s, is a specific case).

And this has an important implication for the pattern of investment fluctuations. Under the conditions of nearly convertible national currency, investment deceleration cannot occur, in Yugoslavia and Hungary it never occurred, without deliberate restrictive measures aimed at breaking investment growth. However, if the national currency is not (even) nearly convertible, then the slowdown may occur despite expansionist investment policy, if the latter is coupled with attempts to improve the foreign trade balance. This means that investment fluctuations tend to be rather irregular if the national currency is not nearly convertible.

Let us look at Graphs 4.1 and 4.2, which display respectively the chain indices of investment outlays in Bulgaria and Hungary in the 1970s. The Hungarian case seems to present relatively regular cycles with a length of 3 to 4 years. In the Bulgarian case we can see irregular fluctuations: there are no real recurrences.

The explanation of these 'nervous' movements of the Bulgarian growth rate, at least partly, is the lack of the Hungarian-Yugoslav kind

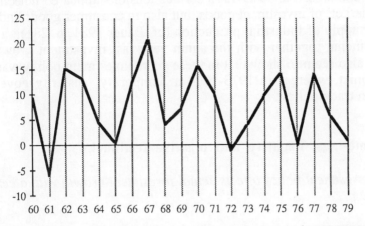

Graph 4.1 - Hungarian Investment Growth (yearly growth rates), 1960-1979

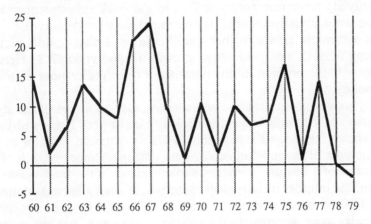

Graph 4.2 - Bulgarian Investment Growth (yearly growth rates), 1960-1979

of quasi-convertibility, in other words, the lack of full harmony between investment and foreign trade policies. For example, the fast investment growth begun in 1972 should have continued in 1973-1974; 10 and 13 per cent increases were planned respectively. But the increase of net machinery imports (imports minus exports) was severely reduced in these years, obviously as a reaction to the deterioration in the foreign trade balance [8], and the investment growth rate dropped to 6.9 and 7.8 per cent in 1973 and 1974 respectively. According to

Bauer's analysis, in 1973-1975 serious tensions appeared not only in the 'market' of investment goods, but also in consumer goods and material supply of industrial production (cf. Bauer 1981, p. 281). These phenomena, together with the again very fast investment growth in 1975, also seem to show that in these years investment policy was expansionist, whereas in 1973-1974 a 'temporary' austerity governed foreign trade policy.

## 2. Time-lags, negative and positive feedbacks

### 2.1. Investment policy affects actual investment growth with a certain time-lag

An important conclusion from division 1. is that investment policy under conditions of quasi-convertibility is always effective: if (and only if) fast growth is stimulated, then actual growth is (or remains) fast; if (and only if) economic policy strives to cut back investment growth then the latter actually becomes (or remains) slow (or negative).

This statement needs further qualifications. I shall come back to clarifying what is 'fast' and 'slow' growth in subdivision 2.3. Here let me stay with the problem of the time-lag of the effectiveness of investment policy.

If anybody begins to analyse actual cases, the soundness of the above conclusion will soon become doubtful for him or her. Let me just stop at the above mentioned Hungarian 1967. Investment policies in this year, the year of the most rapid (22 per cent) investment growth of the last quarter of a century, were not expansionist. In the final version of the plan, the number of new project-starts was nearly halved compared to the draft prepared earlier (cf. Bauer 1981, p. 141); the atmosphere of austerity grew stronger in the course of the year. Let me mention another case. In May 1960, the Yugoslav government introduced credit restrictions [9], and later in the year other measures, in order to cut back investment growth, which nevertheless accelerated, to 19.0 per cent, compared to 14.5 per cent in the previous year.

These ostensible irregularities are in actual fact regularities: government policies affect real investment growth with a certain time-lag. On the basis of annual data, we find that actual investment growth for one year tends to be influenced by the previous year's plan and policy as much as by the plan and policy of the given year (for a summary analysis of this lags functioning during the 1970s in Hungary see Soós 1983). In Soós 1986, on the basis of a quarter-to-quarter (to the extent it was possible month-to-month) analysis I found that the time-lag in question for Hungary and Yugoslavia is one half to one year.

Only weather anomalies (mainly some exceptionally cold winters) make exceptions to this rule (and even then only for some months), otherwise it is absolute. Thus in Hungary and Yugoslavia (i.e. under the conditions of nearly convertible national currency) if investment policy becomes expansionist, then after half to one year actual investment growth becomes fast. On the other hand, if investment policy becomes restrictive, then after half to one year actual investment growth becomes slow (or negative).

This rather short time-lag does not seem to support the crucial role of the completion of started investment projects in investment cycles. According to the latter idea, which appeared in Bauer's analysis of investment cycles of CMEA countries (Bauer 1978) and has become widely accepted, the time pattern of investment accelerations is based on the completion of the started projects. With expansionist policies many new projects are started, which require (in next years) increasing outlays, and this leads to investment peaks. The trouble with this theory is that the completion (gestation) period of investment in ESE's is hopelessly long: the literature usually mentions a period of 4 to 6 years. At the same time, accelerated investment growth in Hungary (the only CMEA country in which investment fluctuations have a relatively clear time regularity) never lasts longer than two years. Thus we have to conclude that suspensions of the completion of started investment projects in austerity periods and their re-startings with expansionist policies, which, of course, are not left out of consideration by Bauer, play a bigger role in actual developments than in the author's theory. Because of this, the macro-level time-lag is not one emanating from the completion of complex investment projects, but one reflecting the slowness of reaction of the production (and the import) of individual investment goods to demand.

Let me explain the difference through an example. If the construction of a new factory is started, the machinery for it may seem to be necessary four years later. But that is irrelevant. During these years austerity policy may appear. Thus the completion of the project may be suspended with an administrative decision (under traditional central planning), or more severe fiscality may deprive the enterprise from the money necessary to buy the machinery (in Hungary or Yugoslavia). Yet sooner or later a new investment drive comes, the production (or the import) of the machinery may be ordered. Then it will be executed within half to one year. (In actual fact even that lag is often much

71

more, but the relatively short delays of production and delivery of standard investment goods determine the macro-level time-lag).

The time-lag holds not only for upswings but also for downswings. It seems to show that the already started production of individual investment goods (as opposed to the completion of the already started complex investment projects) is not usually hurt by the introduction of austerity. I have to add again: under the conditions of nearly convertible national currency.

On this basis, investment fluctuations must have four phases. Namely, between phases of slow and fast growth, as well as between phases of fast and slow growth there have to be transitional or disharmonious phases. In the latter, there is a disharmony between the actual growth rate and the growth rate aimed at by economic policy. The four phases are as follows: *(i)* the run-up phase when economic policy becomes expansionist, but actual investment growth is still slow, or accelerates very slightly; *(ii)* the rush phase in which both the aimed at and the actual growth is fast; *(iii)* the halt phase when economic policy changes towards austerity, but actual investment growth remains fast, or decelerates only very slightly; *(iv)* the setback phase in which the harmony reappears: both the aimed at and the actual growth rate are low (or negative).

Both the idea and the names of the four phases originate from Bauer. Yet the contents of the four phases are somewhat different. The main difference is that in Bauer's model actual investment outlays decelerate already in the third, halt phase. Yet this does not hold for all cycles, and it does not really hold for any of the Hungarian cycles, analysed by him [10]. May be a quarterly or monthly analysis of the processes in the other CMEA countries would produce a different picture. But such an analysis, because of the lack of data (including verbal information) does not seem to be possible (even the author's yearly analysis suffers from lack of data). However, on the basis of available knowledge, I have to suppose that here we again face an irregularity of investment fluctuations under the conditions of the lack of a nearly convertible national currency. This irregularity may be partly identical with the one found in subdivision 1.2.: if the imports of investment goods and materials, semifabricated products used in the domestic production of investment goods are suddenly cut, then investment outlays may decelerate abruptly.

Such sudden cuts, of course, do not happen if the national currency is nearly convertible. Thus, in the latter case, we have clear four-phases investment fluctuations.

## 2.2. Negative feedbacks in 'consumption-symmetrical' and in 'foreign-trade-symmetrical' investment fluctuations

Bauer introduced the distinction between 'consumption-symmetrical' and 'foreign-trade-symmetrical' investment fluctuations. In the former, investments accelerate at the expense of consumption and with investment slowdown consumption accelerates again. In the latter, the foreign trade balance — and not consumption — plays the role of the buffer. Moreover, 'foreign-trade-symmetrical' investment fluctuations tend to be 'consumption-parallel': the growth of consumption accelerates parallel with investment and the growth of consumption is only broken (again together with investment) when economic policy, because of the tension in the balance of foreign trade, is forced to introduce austerity. Obviously, the foreign trade symmetry of investment fluctuations, if it consistently prevails during a longer period, is not only an economic but also a socio-political characteristic of a socialist country.

Investment fluctuations in the 1950s were mostly consumption-symmetrical. From the 1960s on they had a 'mixed' character in most countries, and were definitely foreign-trade-symmetrical in Bulgaria, and in the seventies in Poland (cf. Bauer 1981). The Hungarian and Yugoslav cases also show consistent foreign trade symmetry.

'Symmetry' in this context also implies regulation. In consumption-symmetrical cycles consumption, in foreign-trade-symmetrical cycles the foreign trade balance is the 'regulator'. Regulation means here negative feedback in the sense used in control theory. If the fast growth of investments brings about a deceleration or absolute reduction of consumption or a deterioration of the foreign trade balance exceeding a certain zone which is thought by the central planners to be an equilibrium zone, then this fact enforces the cutback of investment growth. On the other hand, if the development of the 'regulator' is more favorable than desired by the central planners, then a new investment drive begins.

Abstracting from mixed cases, we face here four types of central planners' decisions (two possible outcomes as a reaction to two possible 'regulators'). According to Wiles, three of them may be taken by the leadership on economic grounds, but one, starting an investment drive on the basis of an 'above-the-norm' level of consumption, does not exist. Instead of this the author speaks of an 'external political (investment) peak', brought about by central planners' voluntaristic decision-making (cf. above). .

73

Is starting an investment drive on this basis and doing the same thing on the basis of an 'above-the-norm' improvement of the foreign trade balance so radically different? Theoretically, I think, there are two important differences between the two cases. First, an unwanted improvement of the foreign trade balance is an obvious loss for the socialist planner: resources which could be used for the increase of domestic production are used abroad. An unwanted increase in consumption (instead of which investments could be increased) is not such an obvious loss. Second, if the foreign trade balance is the regulator, then formal calculations concerning future level of indebtedness, interests and instalments to pay, etc. can be made. Whereas the planners' expectations connected to alternative levels of consumption (satisfaction of the population vs. deteriorating work discipline, unrest, etc.) are at least difficult to quantify.

I do not think that any of these differences would be really radical. With regard to the first one, of course, no increase in consumption is an obvious loss for the planners. But, as is described by Olivera 1960 and Bajt 1971, in a centrally planned economy only the planners can and have to represent the interests of investment growth (future consumption) *vis-à-vis* the population, thus a relative improvement of the positions of consumption at some point has to run up against the planners' investment strivings (in Olivera's words, their 'lower time preference'). But at which point does it have to occur? This question leads to the second of the above-mentioned differences. The unquantifiable expectations of the planners cannot provide any obvious answer to this question. However, the case of the other regulator is not really much better. Expectation connected to the foreign trade balance may be quantified, but there is much uncertainty in the data (e.g. in expected future interest rates, etc.), and different indicators (e.g. debt service/exports, growth rate of debts/growth rate of national income, etc.) may be calculated, and they may suggest different reactions. Thus foreign-trade-symmetrical investment policies of central planners are also voluntaristic, or in other words political. Of course not to the same extent as their consumption-symmetrical investment policies. As a matter of fact, political factors tended to synchronise investment policies of different ESE's at a the time of consumption-symmetrical fluctuations in the 1950s. As Wiles says, the Hungarian events of 1956 led to investment cutbacks and accelerated increase of consumption in several countries. And then, under the effect of the Chinese 'Great Leap Forward', ambitious investment plans spread all over Eastern Europe in 1958. But even so, these decisions were not 'purely political', without any economic basis, precisely because the fluctuations had already been synchronised by earlier synchronised decisions. ( For instance, in the 1958 upswing, apart from the Chinese example, the effects of the 1956 cutback also played a certain role).

Leaving the purely theoretical analysis, I have to point out that, according to Bauer's thorough analysis, purely consumption-symmetrical investment fluctuations disappeared in Eastern Europe in the 1960s. In other words, important changes of investment policies after 1960 were always more or less connected with the developments of foreign trade balances. Yet of course, these changes remained somewhat less determined by the circumstances, in this sense more voluntaristic, in those countries where the investment fluctuations did not become purely foreign-trade-symmetrical.

Here we face another factor of time irregularities of investment fluctuations. Let me remind the reader: none of such factors found up to now is relevant for Hungary and Yugoslavia.

*2.3. 'Atmospheres', 'campaigns' as methods of central control and as positive feedback in investment fluctuations*

As Barry Ickes (1986) states, cumulative movements are the most important characteristic of cyclical movements. So whether there are or there are not cumulative movements in investment fluctuations is a crucial problem for judging whether there are investment cycles in ESE's.

This is a rather complicated problem. Fast investment growth is brought about by central planners' decisions. Do they behave cumulatively, that is, do they go on stimulating fast investment growth? I.e., in the terms of control theory, does their behaviour include positive feedback?

A simple positive answer to this question may imply elementary irrationality of the central planners, which obviously would be a poor explanation of more or less regular economic (or political) phenomena. This is probably the reason why Wiles, who otherwise does not have a high opinion of planners' rationality (cf. Wiles, 1962) describes fluctuations as processes often leading to 'stability in moderation'.

In Bauer's model, the investment hunger of firms, ministries, etc. (the 'pressure from below') is the main cumulative factor, the reason for durable and excessive investment accelerations. However I think that the powerlessness of the central planners is not a better explanation than the above-mentioned elementary irrationality. If central planners are capable of executing investment cutbacks (which they certainly are), then they might be capable of hampering excessive investment accelerations, provided they wanted to.

A further problem is that some positive feedback also seems to occur in downswings. In Yugoslavia, austerity measures often lead to dramatic drops in investment outlays (though only for some months, then the policy changes). And in Hungary, for example, the 1972 trough was significantly deeper than was planned: investment outlays, instead of having zero growth, fell by 1.7 per cent in comparison to the 1971 level which was already lower than had been foreseen during the elaboration of the plan for 1972.

The positive feedback in downswings cannot originate from enterprise, etc. behaviour. Thus we have to search for it in the planners' behaviour. My explanation is as follows.

The central control of a planned economy, e.g. of the growth rate of investment outlays, is a very difficult and complicated job. Subordinate levels would like to increase their investments beyond all possible limits. In order to avoid this, physical planning and financial regulation, with their innumerable institutions, are created. Control works then, but rather slowly, through long and inert burocratic channels. Because of this, there are specific difficulties in the implementation of changed policies. Such a changed policy may be an investment acceleration or deceleration. Thus a further, and faster, control device is obviously necessary. And this is a 'general atmosphere', a 'campaign'. Joseph Berliner's early classic book (1957) already analysed the important role of such informal methods in socialist economic control.

An atmosphere of investment acceleration encourages, its counterpart discourages investors. Let me remark that through such control devices 'fine tuning' can hardly be implemented. Thus a policy aiming at 12 per cent yearly growth of investment outlays will probably not result in an actual 12 per cent growth. But if we suppose that 6 per cent is the long term average, then the outcome will be 10, 15 or 20 per cent, in any case more than the long term average, and in this sense 'fast'.

But let us come back to the central planners. How does the atmosphere created by them influence their own behaviour? The atmosphere, as an efficient control device, has to be unambiguous. An atmosphere of investment acceleration would be disturbed if warnings against the dangers of such a trend could be heard. Then the policy to be followed would not be clear for subordinate levels. Experts foreseeing future consequences are in a difficult situation: they are not, nobody is, supposed to contradict the 'right line of action'. Atmospheres, campaigns also create appropriate ideologies. In downswings much is spoken about 'harmony', 'equilibrium', whereas in upswings the 'law of faster growth of the production of the means of production' and the like prevail. The atmosphere leads to a certain kind of loss of collective memory on the part of the central planners.

Thus the atmosphere tends to perpetuate the once begun 'line of action' (cf. Soós 1985). This is a positive feedback in the sense used in control theory. Policies tend to lead to extremities. In upswings, foreign trade deficit increases until it reaches a critical level. In downswings, export surpluses in the trade of machinery with socialist countries accumulate [11]; and although shortages do not disappear, more and more producers of investment goods face difficulties in realisation [12].

The outcome of these processes is rather irrational, but without elementary irrationality in anybody's individual behaviour. Yet the actors of economic policy do not have to be unable to hamper this sequence of events. The 1960-1961 investment cutback in Yugoslavia was certainly a campaign, but the one of 1965 was different, and in 1966, with subsequent small changes of investment policies, 'fine tuning' (in Wiles' words, 'stability in moderation') seemed to appear.

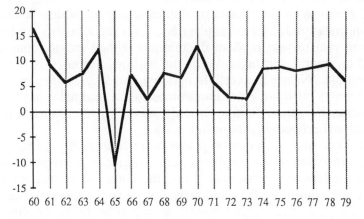

Graph 4.3 - Yugoslav Investment Growth (yearly growth rates), 1960-1979

Then again in 1969, the unfolding investment boom was, long before the appearance of critical foreign trade deficit, curbed by moderately restrictive credit policy. Although these strivings proved to be temporary both (and some other) times, they nevertheless 'disturbed' the regularity of fluctuations. Consequently, Yugoslav investment fluctuations are not regular cycles (see Graph 4.3).

As I come to the end of my paper, I have arrived at a model of regular cyclical fluctuations in which positive and negative feedbacks succeed each other rather regularly. But in the previous paragraph I lost even Yugoslavia and remain with a sole country, Hungary which, as Wiles states,

'was a fertile field... for orthodox economists'.


## 3. Conclusions and the hungarian 'investment boom' of 1985-1986

I think, we can call 'investment cycles' investment fluctuations with systematic successions of negative and positive feedback processes and a minimal amount of regularity in time.

It does not sound very seriously that cycles in this sense are only possible in existing socialist economies in such circumstances in which they are rather unlikely to occur. But it is true. The preconditions of such cycles tend to contradict each other.

Let me clarify some contradictions.

(a) Because of the inertia of domestic supply which is not fully known (measured) by central planners, investment booms are likely to become year-to-year random fluctuations if they are not consistently based on import surpluses, i.e. if the national currency is not nearly convertible. Nearly convertible national currency *eo ipso* means that the planners attribute great importance to the internal equilibrium of the national economy and to the role played by international trade in the national economy (subdivision 1.2.).

Is it likely that such central planners are consistently, in subsequent waves, governed by 'atmospheres', i.e. continue with investment drives which create severe tensions both on the domestic market and in foreign trade equilibrium? Obviously not. The Yugoslav repeated attempts at getting rid of this 'model' seems to be the likely alternative. And that, without avoiding fluctuations, excludes the regular succession of cycles.

(b) Another contradiction is the fact that countries with nearly convertible national currency, which otherwise might have regular cyclical investment fluctuations, are specifically exposed to international economic shocks. These shocks may sometimes coincide with domestic effects. Thus in 1975-1976 Hungarian investment growth had to be cut

78

back for internal reasons; the external shock as another reason for the same action did not disturb the sequence of events. But such coincidences may not be regular; as Mihàlyi says, external shocks influence the fluctuations, tending to synchronise them in various ESE's.

(c) A further contradiction is that an economy which is largely managed by central directives and 'atmospheres', 'campaigns' and which at the outset may be characterised by the inertia of its production (supply), will probably not be able to restore its foreign trade equilibrium during investment slowdowns: less foreign-trade-symmetrical investment fluctuations, in a series of ESE's, amounted in fact to increasing indebtedness in subsequent waves, leaving less and less possibilities for further waves.

Should we then forget the results of research on cycles in socialist economies? No. Even if Hungary was an exceptional case with its unlikely combination of the contradictory preconditions of regular cyclical fluctuations, nothing from what we found in that country was a real 'Hungarian speciality' completely alien to any other country and with no contribution to make towards an understanding of economic policies and economic processes.

And in Hungary, the 'model' is strong. Because of the process mentioned in paragraph (c), it should have disappeared after 1980. But it came back in the second half of 1984. With an improvement of the foreign trade balance and the appearance of some surplus in the balance of payments, an optimism appeared again in the plan for 1985 [13]. After five years of severe (5 to 10 per cent per year) reduction of investment outlays, the drop became slight (2.2 per cent). The deterioration of the proportions of exports and imports in non-rouble trade (the indices were 94.1 and 104.6 per cent, respectively) was explained by random external factors and the optimism, the idea of 'dynamising' the national economy was also included into the plan for 1986 [14]. Thus the 'atmosphere' hampered the recognition of the beginning of a new deterioration of the balance of payments. In 1986, investment growth became slightly positive [15], the increase in consumption was probably somewhat higher than in previous years. This dynamisation in the changed international circumstances and with the unchanged domestic structures, created effects similar to the ones of a real boom in the 1970s. The proportion of non-rouble export and import indices, though partly because of unfavourable changes of prices, further deteriorated (they were 92.5 and 104.3 per cent, respectively). A change towards severe austerity following a 'boom' which was stagnation rather than growth, has become unavoidable.

Obviously, the 'model' has to be changed. But until a new one appears, analysts shall not forget the old one.

## Notes

REMARK: Yugoslav statistical data without references to sources originate from Yugoslav statistical yearbooks. Similar Hungarian data originate from Hungarian statistical yearbooks and from Statisztikai Havi Közlemènyek, 1987, No. 1. The source of the data used in preparing Graph 1 is Bauer (1981).

[1]   Some recent Hungarian university text-books recognise the existence of the cyclical fluctuations in question.

[2]   If there are no domestic resources for the increase of investment expenditures, it does not mean that the production is (in accordance with the views of Jànos Kornai, Josef Goldmann, and many other economists) "resource-constrained". I agree with those analysts who think that firms in the given economic system are not interested in mobilising — and what is more, they are interested in not mobilising — their reserves, they keep back their performance (because of the ratchet principle and other reasons). Cfr. Soòs (1984).

[3]   The export/PNI ratio was in 1967 and 1978 3.9 and 8 per cent in the USSR, 28 and 40 in Bulgaria, 40 and 54 in Hungary, respectively. It was 20 and 31 per cent in Poland, 22 and 30 in the GDR, 17 and 27 in Romany, 30 and 29 in Czechoslovakia in the same years, cfr. Lavigne (1985).

[4]   The comparison between Yugoslavia and other ESEs is difficult because of the differences in national accounting systems, and the necessary Yugoslav data are scarce. In the average of 1968, 1970 and 1972, export sales of industry amounted to 14.7 per cent of all industrial sales in Yugoslavia. The analogous figure for Hungary was 21.1 per cent. On the other hand, invisible Yugoslav exports have been since the middle of the 1960s between 1/6 and 1/3 of the exports of goods (see OECD Economic Surveys. Yugoslavia 1970, 1972 and issues of more recent years).

[5]   Cf. A nèpgazdasàg 1970. èvi terve (The national economic plan for 1970), Nèpszabadsàg, 14 December 1969; A nèpgazdasàg 1974. èvi terve (The national economic plan for 1974), *Nèpszabadsàg*, 19 December 1976.

[6] Cf. OECD Economic Surveys. Yugoslavia, Paris, 1974.

[7] Cf. Rezolucija o osnovama politike drustveno-ekonomskog razvoja u 1970. godini (Resolution on the bases of socio-economic policy in 1970), Sluzbeni list SFRJ 1969 No. 56.

[8] The foreign trade balance displayed a surplus of 202 million devise levas in 1970, which diminished to 73 millions in 1971, to 65 and 29 millions in 1972 and 1973, respectively. In 1974 a high deficit (475 millions) appeared which was obviously connected with the bad crop and the well-known changes in international trade. Source: Bauer (1981), p. 281.

[9] Cf.Krediti i rezerve (Credits and reserves), *Ekonomska politika*, 14 May 1960.

[10] According to the author's analysis, 1960, 1964, and — the last year of his analysis — 1967 are halts. Although we do see some deceleration in the first two cases, the third represents an important acceleration. The chain indices (also displayed in figure 1) are: 1958: 29.0, 1959: 35.9, 1960: 11.0, 1961: –6.9, 1962: 15.5, 1963: 13.2, 1964: 4.8, 1965: 0.4, 1966: 11.5, 1967: 22.0 per cent. Later, years of halts were 1971 with 9.7 p.c. increase of investment expenditure (between 16.7 in 1970 and –1.7 in 1972); 1975 (14.4 p.c., preceded by 9.5 in 1974, and followed by –0.3 in 1976); and 1978 (5.5 p.c., after 14.4 in 1977 and before 1.1 in 1979). Cf. Soós (1986).

[11] As it occurred in Hungary in 1968-1969, see J. Fày: Folytatòdik a külkereskedelmi expanziò (Foreign trade expansion continues), *Figyelö*, 2 September 1970.

[12] For instance in the Yugoslav engineering industry in 1972-1973; see: Procesna oprema. Kapaciteti su prednost (Productive machinery. Capacities mean advantage), *Ekonomska politika*, 9 July 1973.

[13] Bagota B. – Garam J.: Mit kell tudni az 1985. èvi nèpgazdasàgi tervröl? (What is to be known about the national economic plan for 1985?), Budapest, Kossuth, 1985.

[14] Bagota B. – Garam J.: Mit kell tudni a hetedik ötèves tervröl? (What is to be known about the seventh five-year plan?), Budapest, Kossuth, 1986.

[15] Investment outlays increased at current prices by 5.0 per cent. The only here rationally appliable price index which is already available in March 1987 is that of industrial production –2.0 per cent. The investment price index cannot be much more, therefore real investment growth was very probably positive.

# References

Bajt, A. (1971), 'Investment Cycles in Socialist Economies: a Review Article', *The Journal of Economic Literature*, vol. 9, no.1.
— (1972), *Anatomija zunanjetrgovinskega primanjkljaja* (The anatomy of the foreign trade deficit), Ekonomski institut Pravne fakultete, Liubljana.
Bauer, T. (1978), 'Investment Cycles in Planned Economies', *Acta Œconomica*, vol. 21, no. 3.
— (1981), *Tervgazdasàg, beruhàzàs, ciklusok* (Planned economy, investment, cycles), KJK, Budapest.
Berliner, J.S. (1957), *Factory and Manager in the USSR*, Harvard University Press, Cambridge (Mass.).
Horvat, B. (1971), 'Business Cycles in Yugoslavia', *Eastern European Economics*, vol. 9, no. 3-4.
Ickes, B.W. (1986), 'Cyclical Fluctuations in Centrally Planned Economies: a Critique of the Literature', *Soviet Studies*, vol. 37, no. 1.
Kovac, O. (1973), 'Spoljnoekonomska ravnoteza i privredni rast. Problemi i iskustva Jugoslavije' (Foreign trade equilibrium and economic growth. The problems and experiences of Yugoslavia), *Œconomica*, Belgrade.
Lavigne, M. (1985), *Economie internationale des pays socialistes*, Armand Colin, Paris.
Mihàlyi, P. (1986), *The Synchronization of Investment Fluctuations in Eastern Europe (1950-1985)*, paper submitted to the international conference 'Régulation, cycles et crises dans les économies socialistes', organised by the Ecole des Hautes Etudes en Sciences Sociales in Paris, 13-14 March.
Olivera, J.H.G. (1960), 'Cyclical Economic Growth under Collectivism', *Kyklos*, no. 2.
Podolski, T.M. (1973), *Socialist Banking and Monetary Control. The Experience of Poland*, Cambridge University Press, Cambrige.
Soòs, K.A. (1983), 'The Problem of Time-Lags in the Short-Term Control of Macroeconomic Processes', *Acta Œconomica*, vol. 30, no. 3-4.
— (1984), 'A propos the Explanation of Shortage Phenomena: Volume of Demand and Structural Inelasticity', *Acta Œconomica*, vol. 33, no. 3-4.
— (1985), 'Planification impérative, régulation financière, 'grandes orientations' et campagnes' *Revue d'Etudes Comparatives Est-Ouest*, vol. 16, no. 2.

— (1986), *Terv, kampàny, pènz. Szabàlyozàs ès konjunjturaciklusok Magyarorszàgon ès Jugoszlàviàban* (Plan, campaign, money. Regulation and cycles in Hungary and Yugoslavia), KJK, Budapest.

Wiles, P.J.D. (1962), *The Political Economy of Communism*, Basil Blackwell, Oxford.

— (1981), 'Are There Any Communist Economic Cycles?' *The ACES Bulletin*, vol. 24, no. 2.

# 5  Common patterns and particularities in East European investment cycles

PETER MIHÁLYI

## 1. Introduction

The main purpose of this paper is to attempt a cross-country analysis of investment cycles [1]. Three objectives are intended to be met.

(a) To present data in a systematic manner, drawn from computerised data bases, for a small sample of the cycles experienced by six east European countries. This approach will provide us with an approximate measuring instrument, whereby the changes in relevant macro-economic variables in country 'A' can be quantitatively assessed in comparison with the behaviour of the same variables in the other five countries.

b) To perform a rough consistency check on the widely used data. It is assumed that certain macro-variables should meet certain coherency criteria in a national accounting sense (e.g. growing investments plus growing consumption requires a rise in domestic utilisation of national income).

(c) To draw attention to common behavioural patterns during the cycles, but also to significant time and country specific differences among them.

In Section 2, the volume of annual gross domestic investments (henceforth GINV) is treated as an exogenous control variable in the

84

hands of the planners. The objective is to focus on the immediate, short term consequences of fluctuations in GINV. Some of our results confirm the findings of earlier research concerning the typical response of cycle-relevant variables (e.g. construction, machinery imports), but in other cases (e.g. trade balance, allocation of NMP) we have found surprisingly little evidence for any systematic behaviour [2]. Finally, in Section 3 the role of agricultural harvest fluctuations will also be briefly touched upon - an issue which is usually not taken into serious consideration in the socialist investment cycle theory.

By way of introduction, it should be emphasised that throughout this study the term 'investment cycle' is used in a broad, non-econometric sense. Controversial issues of empirical nature, like time regularity of fluctuations, as well as international synchronisation of cycles are completely disregarded here [3].

Apart from a few exceptions, forced upon us by data constraints, the analysis was conducted in terms of annual growth rates (expressed in percentage form) at constant prices [4]. For each of the six east European economies (Bulgaria, Czechoslovakia, the German Democratic Republic, Hungary, Poland and Romania) one and only one period was chosen. In the selection, the following criteria were applied.

(i) A cycle consists of two or three years of marked acceleration of GINV, preceded and followed by one or two years of conspicuously restrained or negative investment growth.

(ii) Those years were excluded from the investigation, when the country in question was hit by a sizeable adverse external shock or by a major domestic political crisis. For this reason, as well as due to data availability constraints, the first 15 years of socialist development (1945-1960) were not analysed [5]. The years after 1973, when dramatic changes in relative world market prices disadvantageously affected five countries out of six, were represented in our sample by Poland -i. e. by the only country of the region that benefited from these changes. For the other five economies, the cycles were chosen from the 'normal' and 'peaceful' period between 1960-1973.

(iii) Out of ten clearly discernible GINV cycles, those six were selected which had the highest peaks. Thus four cases were omitted: two in Hungary (1965-1967-1968, 1968-1970-1972), one in Bulgaria (1961-1963-1965) and one in Poland (1963-1967-1970) [6].

For the purposes of this exercise, 32 different macro variables were chosen in order to depict the consequences of the investment cycle in the entire economy. Some of these variables served only for control purposes (e.g. mirror statistics of partner countries in foreign trade), some others proved to be irrelevant in the course of the investigation. All these figures were deliberately retained in Tables 5.1-5.6, for the sake of completeness, but their message was often not analysed in the text. To our regret, two rather important areas remained in the shadows. First, restrictive policy measures are generally explained and defended - at the time of their introduction - as a necessary response to changes in the debt situation, or in the balance-of-payments. Secondly, it is known from anecdotal evidences, that national defence considerations were often decisive motives behind the investment upswing. Unfortunately, none of these countries publish adequate debt or balance-of-payment figures for the years prior to 1970 and even less is known about defence policy decisions.

Given the short term nature of the investment cycles, as well as the factors mentioned above in paragraph (ii), econometric measurement methods were not applied in the analysis. Thus - at least at this stage of research - we had to content ourselves with qualitative statements concerning the strength of association between changes in cycle relevant variables.

## Six countries - six cycles

Given the large share of <u>construction work</u> involved in the investment process - ranging between 42 per cent (GDR) and 64 per cent (Czechoslovakia) in the years of our cycles -, it seems to be appropriate to start our investigation in this area. In Table 5.1 three variables were displayed: employment in and net output of the construction sector, as well as gross output of the construction materials-producing branch of industry.

It can be observed that <u>the upswing in investments was in general strongly associated with a noticeable rise in the construction work variables</u>, Hungary and Poland being the exceptions. Employment showed a vigorous adjustment to the growing demand for construction work almost everywhere. As for employment growth, the picture was similar in Poland, too. In this regard, the development in Hungary was unique: after a short lived surge in 1962, employment appears to have really started to expand only when the investment boom was already over [7].

86

Table 5.1
Total investments and the performance of the construction branches (Annual percentage change)

|  | Years | GINV | EMPC | CONST(N) | CONSTMAT |
|---|---|---|---|---|---|
| HUNGARY | 1961 | -1.1 | 0.9 | 2.2 | 5.8 |
|  | 1962 | 10.0 | 5.8 | 2.3 | 2.4 |
|  | 1963 | 15.5 | 0.9 | 3.6 | 2.1 |
|  | 1964 | 3.3 | 0.6 | 4.2 | 5.1 |
|  | 1965 | 1.3 | 13.1 | 0.7 | 4.2 |
| CZECHOSLOVAKIA | 1963 | -11.2 | -2.7 | -15.6 | -8.7 |
|  | 1964 | 11.1 | 0.7 | 12.3 | 7.1 |
|  | 1965 | 7.5 | 2.4 | 13.0 | 9.0 |
|  | 1966 | 9.5 | 3.9 | 19.0 | 7.9 |
|  | 1967 | 3.0 | 3.0 | 7.3 | 8.2 |
| BULGARIA | 1965 | 7.4 | 3.3 | 2.8 | 11.0 |
|  | 1966 | 19.6 | 6.5 | 16.1 | 17.0 |
|  | 1967 | 23.6 | 5.3 | 16.7 | 13.0 |
|  | 1968 | 9.0 | 4.6 | 14.4 | 10.0 |
|  | 1969 | 1.0 | -2.5 | 5.3 | 4.0 |
| ROMANIA | 1965 | 9.0 | 2.3 | 5.2 | 14.0 |
|  | 1966 | 9.9 | 7.0 | 8.0 | 9.0 |
|  | 1967 | 16.6 | 11.1 | 14.6 | 14.0 |
|  | 1968 | 11.7 | 4.2 | 13.5 | 17.0 |
|  | 1969 | 6.6 | 2.1 | 7.3 | 12.0 |
| G. D. R. | 1966 | 6.9 | 0.5 | 7.3 | 5.0 |
|  | 1967 | 9.3 | 1.0 | 5.8 | 4.0 |
|  | 1968 | 11.0 | 8.1 | 11.4 | 6.0 |
|  | 1969 | 16.0 | 5.7 | 7.6 | 2.0 |
|  | 1970 | 7.0 | 3.3 | 4.9 | 13.0 |
|  | 1971 | 1.3 | 1.7 | 4.7 | 6.0 |
| POLAND | 1970 | 4.0 | 0.4 | 3.3 | 6.0 |
|  | 1971 | 7.4 | 4.4 | 5.0 | 6.7 |
|  | 1972 | 23.0 | 6.5 | 21.4 | 8.6 |
|  | 1973 | 25.4 | 10.2 | 16.3 | 8.0 |
|  | 1974 | 22.3 | 7.5 | 13.7 | 8.6 |
|  | 1975 | 10.7 | 1.0 | 11.0 | 8.7 |
|  | 1976 | 1.0 | -1.2 | 2.5 | 5.8 |
|  | 1977 | 3.1 | -0.3 | 1.0 | 4.1 |
|  | 1978 | 2.1 | 0.3 | -0.3 | 2.1 |
|  | 1979 | -7.9 | -1.6 | -6.2 | -4.6 |

Labels: GINV      = Total gross investments
       EMPC     = Employment in the construction sector.
       COST(N)   = Net output of the construction sector.
       CONSTMAT = Gross output of the construction material producing branch.

Source: ECE Common Data Base, derived from national or CMEA statistics.

## Table 5.2
## Total investments and the performance of industry
### (Annual percentage change)

| | Year | GINV | INDT | IND(A) | XSOC | XSOCMACH | XNSOC | XNSMACH |
|---|---|---|---|---|---|---|---|---|
| HUNGARY | | | | | | | | |
| | 1961 | 1.1 | 8.3 | 12.3 | 21.8 | 18.5 | 9.6 | 3.0 |
| | 1962 | 10.0 | 7.0 | 11.0 | 5.8 | 3.4 | 10.4 | 48.2 |
| | 1963 | 15.5 | 6.7 | 5.9 | 4.2 | 0.1 | 27.6 | 25.3 |
| | 1964 | 3.3 | 7.1 | 9.3 | 13.0 | 24.3 | 5.0 | 34.3 |
| | 1965 | 1.3 | 4.0 | 5.1 | 11.4 | 9.1 | 24.0 | 17.1 |
| CZECHOSLOVAKIA | 1963 | -11.2 | -0.6 | -1.1 | 12.4 | 14.9 | 1.6 | -7.3 |
| | 1964 | 11.1 | 4.1 | 5.1 | 3.1 | 2.5 | 20.1 | 4.9 |
| | 1965 | 7.5 | 7.9 | 9.2 | 2.9 | 5.8 | 9.4 | 14.9 |
| | 1966 | 9.5 | 7.4 | 8.2 | 0.1 | 1.0 | 19.4 | 30.9 |
| | 1967 | 3.0 | 7.1 | 7.5 | 7.8 | 6.0 | 1.0 | -10.7 |
| BULGARIA | 1965 | 7.4 | 14.7 | 16.8 | 17.7 | 39.7 | 15.0 | 30.9 |
| | 1966 | 19.6 | 12.2 | 12.8 | 9.2 | 15.0 | 28.5 | 4.8 |
| | 1967 | 23.6 | 13.3 | 14.1 | 13.4 | 17.5 | 11.3 | 39.1 |
| | 1968 | 9.0 | 10.1 | 10.6 | 11.6 | 17.4 | 12.2 | 56.1 |
| | 1969 | 1.0 | 9.4 | 9.9 | 9.6 | 15.5 | 5.5 | 21.2 |
| ROMANIA | 1965 | 9.0 | 13.1 | 13.7 | 9.8 | 3.7 | 13.0 | 18.4 |
| | 1966 | 9.9 | 11.4 | 12.4 | -5.4 | 2.8 | 39.6 | 41.7 |
| | 1967 | 16.6 | 13.6 | 14.3 | 12.6 | 12.1 | 29.8 | 39.0 |
| | 1968 | 11.7 | 11.7 | 14.1 | 7.3 | 11.7 | -1.5 | 15.2 |
| | 1969 | 6.6 | 10.6 | 10.3 | 17.3 | 12.2 | 11.7 | 24.7 |
| G.D.R. | 1966 | 6.9 | 6.5 | 6.2 | 6.2 | 2.3 | 9.1 | 11.0 |
| | 1967 | 9.3 | 6.8 | 7.2 | 11.0 | 13.3 | 4.8 | 7.2 |
| | 1968 | 11.0 | 5.9 | 6.7 | 10.7 | 12.4 | 1.8 | 5.1 |
| | 1969 | 16.0 | 6.9 | 8.7 | 3.7 | 4.6 | 30.3 | 29.8 |
| | 1970 | 7.0 | 6.7 | 7.7 | 9.9 | 7.2 | -0.1 | 11.3 |
| | 1971 | 1.3 | 5.7 | 6.4 | 12.4 | 11.4 | 2.4 | 13.4 |
| POLAND | 1970 | 4.0 | 8.1 | 9.0 | 9.0 | 15.7 | - | 40.6 |
| | 1971 | 7.4 | 7.9 | 8.3 | 10.1 | 2.6 | 9.1 | 26.2 |
| | 1972 | 23.0 | 10.7 | 10.6 | 13.7 | 13.0 | 12.6 | 18.5 |
| | 1973 | 25.4 | 11.2 | 11.6 | 12.4 | 16.9 | 14.6 | 9.3 |
| | 1974 | 22.3 | 11.4 | 12.0 | 14.0 | 19.2 | 18.4 | 26.3 |
| | 1975 | 10.7 | 10.9 | 10.7 | 10.8 | 13.2 | 5.5 | 39.7 |
| | 1976 | 1.0 | 9.3 | 9.7 | -1.1 | -0.5 | 7.8 | 9.6 |
| | 1977 | 3.1 | 6.9 | 6.4 | 10.0 | 12.1 | 5.6 | 10.4 |
| | 1978 | 2.1 | 4.9 | 4.4 | 5.6 | 5.9 | 1.6 | 7.0 |
| | 1979 | -7.9 | 2.7 | 2.6 | 8.8 | 16.6 | 2.2 | 0.3 |

Labels: GINV      = Total gross investments
        INDT      = Gross industrial output
        IND(A)    = Output in sector 'A'   (Hungary: Heavy industry without mining)
        XSOC      = Non-agricultural exports into the socialist countries
        XSOCMACH = Machinery exports into socialist countries
        XNSOC    = Non-agricultural exports into non-socialist countries
        XNSMACH = Machinery exports into non-socialist countries

Source: ECE Common Data Base, derived from national or CMEA statistics; United Nations commodity trade data (COMTRADE) and Statistisches Bundesamt, Warenverkehr mit der Deutschen Demokratischen Republik und Berlin (Ost), Reihe 6, Wiesbaden.

In all six countries but Hungary, the behaviour of the net output of the construction sector was parallel to the changes in GINV [8]. Also, rising investments were supported by a dynamic expansion of the construction material branch nearly everywhere. Here, the notable exception was Poland - where the growth rates of the CONSTMAT variable remained practically unchanged despite the trebling of reported GINV rates. The picture was similar but not so marked in the German Democratic Republic. At the peak of the investment cycle, when GINV grew by no less than 16.0 per cent, CONSTMAT showed a very modest 2 per cent growth, down from a 6 per cent annual rate, registered in the previous year; moreover no substantial reversal occurred until 1970, by which time, however, GINV rate had halved.

The performance of industry can also a priori be assumed to be closely linked to the investment cycle. Needless to say, no simple correspondence in growth rates was expected. But since the volume of annual industrial output is about 4-5 times larger than that of GINV, a noticeable, but not necessarily spectacular growth in INDT can, in principle, easily be compatible with a very buoyant rise in GINV (accelerator effect).

In fact, an unquestionably close relationship between the two was found only for Czechoslovakia and Poland (Table 5.2). In Bulgaria, Hungary and Romania, gross industrial output showed a clear decelerating tendency throughout the periods under review, irrespective of what happened in the investment domain. In the German Democratic Republic INDT growth rates were high - but they showed no sign of acceleration as the investment cycle was asserting itself. In fact, the same high, but stable rates (around 6-7 per cent) were reported for INDT for all years in the 1964-1976 period, while the growth rates of investment continued to fluctuate in later years, too (1972-1974: 4.3 per cent, 8.5 per cent,5.5 per cent).

Table 5.2 also offers some information about the performance of the so-called 'Group A' sub-sector of industry (producer goods output) - an indicator closely monitored in many East European countries, and duly reported by the CMEA statistical sources. The findings about the behaviour of INDT, summarised in the previous paragraph hold for this variable, too.

With regard to the export performance of industry, it is generally believed that it behaves anti-cyclically. However, this hypothesis is only supported by data from three countries. In Czechoslovakia, GDR and in Hungary, it was found that a surge in GINV provoked a contraction in machinery exports, and conversely, weakening domestic investment demand allowed (or required) a strengthening of machinery export.

Presumably these developments were causatively related to the cyclical changes in domestic demand, but it would go beyond the purposes of the present paper to verify this train of thought.

Except for the two less developed economies of the region (Bulgaria and Romania) the investment cycle is positively associated with the fluctuations in machinery imports [9]. This finding (Table 5.3) seems to hold both for purchases in socialist and non-socialist countries alike. Mirror data - taken from OECD sources - also confirm this relationship, at least as far as imports from the west are concerned. It is interesting to note, however, that for three countries (Czechoslovakia, GDR and Hungary) machinery imports from non-socialist countries continued to show an acceleration one or two years after the peak in the GINV growth rate. This is all the more surprising, since it is generally believed that long lead times between orders and actual deliveries are typical to intra-CMEA trade, but not of imports originating from the OECD countries. This surprising phenomenon could be explained by the fact that western machinery tends to be used at the end-phase of investment projects. Thus, in times of slowing overall investment growth, when efforts are often concentrated on the completion of projects, western machinery imports continue to grow for one or two years. In Bulgaria, a positive association between machinery imports and the investment cycle can be established only for imports originating in the socialist countries. In this case, but also in Romania, imports of western machinery were allowed to jump only in a single year in the upward phase of the cycle (1966 for Bulgaria, 1967 for Romania). This was followed by an immediate downturn.

It is often argued that major increases in investments are usually coupled with a slow-down in consumption growth, while a moderation of investment growth allows more resources to be allocated for the purpose of improving the supply of material goods to the population. Table 5.4 displays some figures to test this hypothesis. As far as the most aggregate variable - personal consumption of material goods - is concerned, it appears that such a relationship simply does not exist. In fact the evidence points in the opposite direction. Increasing investments go hand in hand with rising private consumption. However, in three cases (Czechoslovakia, GDR, Romania) personal consumption at the peak of the cycle grew at a faster rate than the NMP produced. Thus the textbook example of a trade-off (more guns or more butter) cannot be demonstrated. On the contrary, as soon as the expansion of GINV is curtailed, NMP(PC) growth rates also start to weaken.

Table 5.3
Total investments and imports of machinery
(Annual percentage change)

| | Year | GINV | SOCMACH | NSOCMACH | OECDMACH |
|---|---|---|---|---|---|
| HUNGARY | 1961 | -1.1 | 25.7 | 16.7 | ... |
| | 1962 | 10.0 | 20.5 | 2.3 | ... |
| | 1963 | 15.5 | 12.8 | 24.1 | 26.4 |
| | 1964 | 3.3 | -2.6 | 49.5 | 26.3 |
| | 1965 | 1.3 | -2.2 | 7.7 | -3.7 |
| CZECHOSLOVAKIA | 1963 | -11.2 | -0.1 | 6.1 | -11.5 |
| | 1964 | 11.1 | 26.3 | 20.3 | 13.5 |
| | 1965 | 7.5 | 14.2 | 33.4 | 26.4 |
| | 1966 | 9.5 | 3.6 | 55.7 | 49.0 |
| | 1967 | 3.0 | -6.5 | -15.1 | -9.4 |
| BULGARIA | 1965 | 7.4 | 16.6 | 29.5 | ... |
| | 1966 | 19.6 | 20.0 | 117.2 | 97.4 |
| | 1967 | 23.6 | 10.2 | -10.1 | -6.6 |
| | 1968 | 9.0 | 9.1 | -28.6 | -36.0 |
| | 1969 | 1.0 | -1.4 | -20.3 | -7.7 |
| ROMANIA | 1965 | 9.0 | -17.1 | 20.4 | 24.5 |
| | 1966 | 9.9 | 14.7 | 18.8 | 25.2 |
| | 1967 | 16.6 | 4.2 | 41.4 | 100.3 |
| | 1968 | 11.7 | 12.6 | -7.0 | -5.5 |
| | 1969 | 6.6 | 5.2 | 9.6 | -10.3 |
| G.D.R. | 1966 | 6.9 | 19.7 | 32.9 | 58.5 |
| | 1967 | 9.3 | 26.1 | 6.7 | 7.7 |
| | 1968 | 11.0 | 29.4 | -4.9 | -18.4 |
| | 1969 | 16.0 | 31.0 | 40.8 | 34.0 |
| | 1970 | 7.0 | 5.2 | 58.1 | 29.5 |
| | 1971 | 1.3 | 4.5 | 1.5 | -1.9 |
| POLAND | 1970 | 4.0 | 25.6 | -14.0 | -20.0 |
| | 1971 | 7.4 | -3.6 | 16.8 | 6.1 |
| | 1972 | 23.0 | 17.3 | 88.0 | 66.8 |
| | 1973 | 25.4 | 26.3 | 52.4 | 52.1 |
| | 1974 | 22.3 | 12.9 | 21.7 | 24.3 |
| | 1975 | 10.7 | -4.3 | 18.7 | 12.5 |
| | 1976 | 1.0 | 8.5 | -3.3 | -5.1 |
| | 1977 | 3.1 | 7.1 | -13.7 | -20.0 |
| | 1978 | 2.1 | 6.8 | -9.9 | -15.2 |
| | 1979 | -7.9 | 4.9 | -20.6 | -20.3 |

Labels: GINV  = Total gross investments
SOCMACH = Machinery imports from socialist countries.
NSOCMACH = Machinery imports from non-socialist countries.
OECDMACH = Machinery imports from the OECD countries (SITC 7 at constant 1975 US dollars; Hungary and CSSR: at current US $ prices)

Source: ECE Common Data Base, derived from national or CMEA statistics; United Nations commodity trade data (COMTRADE) and Statistisches Bundesamt, Warenverkehr mit der Deutschen Demokratischen Republik und Berlin (Ost), Reihe 6, Wiesbaden.

SYMBOLS EMPLOYED: ... NOT AVAILABLE
. NOT APPLICABLE
- MAGNITUDE NOT ZERO, BUT LESS THAN HALF OF UNITY EMPLOYED
0 MAGNITUDE ZERO

## Table 5.4
### Total investments and consumption of the population
### (Annual percentage change)

|  | Year | GINV | NMP(PC) | IND(B) | MSOCCON | MNSOCCON | OECDCONS | DWELLING |
|---|---|---|---|---|---|---|---|---|
| HUNGARY | 1961 | -1.1 | 1.1 | 8.5 | 1.3 | 10.6 | ... | 16.3 |
|  | 1962 | 10.0 | 3.4 | 4.1 | 26.0 | 3.0 | ... | -19.9 |
|  | 1963 | 15.5 | 4.7 | 5.0 | 1.1 | 23.3 | 10.6 | -2.5 |
|  | 1964 | 3.3 | 5.4 | 7.6 | -2.7 | -3.7 | 16.8 | 1.3 |
|  | 1965 | 1.3 | 1.5 | 3.6 | 16.1 | -0.7 | 15.8 | 2.2 |
| CZECHOSLOVAKIA | 1963 | -11.2 | 1.1 | 0.1 | -11.9 | 6.3 | - | -3.6 |
|  | 1964 | 11.1 | 3.0 | 2.6 | 5.5 | 30.6 | 37.3 | -5.9 |
|  | 1965 | 7.5 | 5.1 | 5.7 | 47.6 | 73.0 | 35.7 | 0.7 |
|  | 1966 | 9.5 | 5.3 | 5.9 | 17.5 | 39.7 | 26.2 | -2.9 |
|  | 1967 | 3.0 | 3.5 | 6.4 | -10.3 | 11.9 | 9.5 | 5.0 |
| BULGARIA | 1965 | 7.4 | 7.2 | 12.4 | -6.0 | 50.4 | ... | -4.6 |
|  | 1966 | 19.6 | 6.3 | 11.5 | 31.3 | 51.4 | 36.2 | -4.0 |
|  | 1967 | 23.6 | 9.6 | 12.4 | 4.9 | 0.2 | -7.6 | -1.6 |
|  | 1968 | 9.0 | 8.6 | 9.6 | 23.5 | -2.9 | -24.2 | -0.1 |
|  | 1969 | 1.0 | 5.0 | 8.9 | -2.9 | -8.9 | 11.6 | 10.3 |
| ROMANIA | 1965 | 9.0 | 7.9 | 11.5 | -25.0 | 24.8 | 30.0 | ... |
|  | 1966 | 9.9 | 10.4 | 9.8 | 18.2 | 28.6 | 27.5 | -3.0 |
|  | 1967 | 16.6 | 11.0 | 13.1 | 20.8 | 100.2 | 74.7 | 4.0 |
|  | 1968 | 11.7 | 8.9 | 7.7 | -2.2 | 4.1 | 17.4 | -7.0 |
|  | 1969 | 6.6 | 4.7 | 10.1 | 14.5 | -16.0 | 2.1 | 26.0 |
| G.D.R. | 1966 | 6.9 | 4.5 | 7.2 | 35.1 | 7.4 | 6.9 | -8.5 |
|  | 1967 | 9.3 | 3.4 | 6.2 | 11.8 | 13.8 | 25.8 | 10.8 |
|  | 1968 | 11.0 | 4.1 | 4.5 | 11.1 | 2.7 | -21.7 | 4.7 |
|  | 1969 | 16.0 | 5.6 | 1.7 | 25.9 | 84.7 | 63.9 | -8.6 |
|  | 1970 | 7.0 | 3.8 | 3.8 | -2.3 | 8.4 | 22.9 | 16.3 |
|  | 1971 | 1.3 | 3.6 | 4.5 | -1.4 | 9.6 | 10.1 | -1.2 |
| POLAND | 1970 | 4.0 | 4.0 | 7.6 | 36.9 | 162.4 | 6.1 | -1.4 |
|  | 1971 | 7.4 | 7.0 | 8.2 | 14.6 | -41.0 | 23.0 | -1.9 |
|  | 1972 | 23.0 | 8.7 | 11.0 | 16.2 | 79.5 | 36.7 | 7.8 |
|  | 1973 | 25.4 | 8.5 | 10.8 | -8.1 | 23.7 | 23.4 | 10.5 |
|  | 1974 | 22.3 | 6.8 | 10.6 | 11.6 | 11.2 | 23.7 | 10.0 |
|  | 1975 | 10.7 | 11.4 | 11.4 | 18.5 | -13.8 | -4.8 | -0.7 |
|  | 1976 | 1.0 | 8.7 | 8.8 | -2.1 | 40.2 | 28.5 | 6.2 |
|  | 1977 | 3.1 | 6.6 | 7.3 | 23.3 | 3.2 | -13.7 | 1.0 |
|  | 1978 | 2.1 | 1.0 | 5.3 | 8.1 | -24.4 | -5.0 | 6.6 |
|  | 1979 | -7.9 | 3.2 | 2.2 | -1.6 | 23.4 | -14.1 | -2.0 |

Labels: GINV = Total gross investments
IND(B) = Gross output of sector 'B' within industry. (Hungary: Light industry)
NMP(PC) = Personal consumption of material goods. (Romania: Retail trade turnover in the socialist sector)
MSOCCON = Imports of industrial consumer goods from socialist countries.
MNSOCCON = Imports of industrial consumer goods from non-socialist countries.
OECDCONS = Imports of industrial consumer goods from OECD countries.
SITC 8 at constant 1975 US dollars (Hungary and CSSR: at current US $ prices)
DWELLING = Annual dwelling construction (in physical units).

Source: ECE Common Data Base, derived from national or CMEA statistics; United Nations commodity trade data (COMTRADE) and Statistisches Bundesamt, Warenverkehr mit der Deutschen Demokratischen Republik und Berlin (Ost), Reihe 6, Wiesbaden.

SYMBOLS EMPLOYED:     ... NOT AVAILABLE
. NOT APPLICABLE
- MAGNITUDE NOT ZERO, BUT LESS THAN HALF OF UNITY EMPLOYED
0 MAGNITUDE ZERO

The behaviour of the 'Group B' sub-sector of industry (consumer goods) offers no conclusive evidence in either direction. In fact, to some extent it seems to contradict the findings related to the changes in NMP(PC). In the developed economies - Czechoslovakia, GDR and Hungary - changes in output growth of the consumer goods-producing industries were clearly anti-cyclical with respect to fluctuations in GINV, as the textbook example would suggest. On the other hand they were strongly pro-cyclical in Poland. In Bulgaria, the slow-down of output growth seems to be completely independent of GINV, while in Romania, the figures oscillate so widely that no clear relationship can be asserted.

As is well known, imports of consumer goods never amounted to significant volumes. Typically, in the periods under investigation the annual machinery import was 5-10 times higher than the volume of imported consumer goods. Thus it is no wonder that fluctuations in the growth rates of these types of imports are rather independent of changes in GINV. A more uniform picture emerges if the fluctuation in dwelling construction is analysed: apart from Poland, a rather strict anti-cyclical pattern seems to prevail in all countries.

Rapidly growing investments often provoke tension in the allocation of net material product. Out of those four countries for which comparable NMP data at constant prices are available, in three of them (Bulgaria, Hungary and Poland) the peaks in GINV coincide with a significant 'excess spending' (Table 5.5). In other words, the volume of NMP used is greater than the volume of NMP produced. (i.e. domestic demand is greater than domestic output). In this regard, Hungary proved to be the most notorious 'excess spender': in two consecutive years, NMP used surpassed NMP produced by more than 10 per cent. (The absolute record was reached in 1971, when the gap expanded to 18 per cent. No other country - not even Poland in the 1970s, matched this negative record.) [10]. In Czechoslovakia the NMPUT/PR ratio was very close to 100 per cent throughout the entire 1963-1967 period, in spite of considerable variations in GINV. Interestingly, changes in net investments clearly followed GINV. The share of net fixed capital formation in NMP used (FA/UT) peaked in 1964 and dropped in each year thereafter. However, the counter-cyclical direction of changes in stocks (which include the changes in unfinished investments) almost entirely offset its impact on the accumulation ratio. From a longer time perspective, the year 1965 proved to be the absolute trough (17 per cent) for the ACC/UT ratio between to major peaks in 1961 and 1976, when the accumulation ratio was around 26-27 per cent. In the GDR, where information about the utilisation of NMP is

Table 5.5
Total investments and allocations of NMP
(Percentage shares)

| Year | GINV (% change) | NMPUT/PR | ACC/UT | FA/UT | STOCK/UT | M/XSOC | M/XUSSR | M/XOECD | M/XOECDC |
|---|---|---|---|---|---|---|---|---|---|
| **HUNGARY** | | | | | | | | | |
| 1961 | -1.1 | 109.0 | 18.1 | 11.3 | 7.8 | 92.9 | 110.0 | 126.0 | ... |
| 1962 | 10.0 | 109.5 | 18.5 | 11.4 | 8.1 | 101.4 | 105.7 | 113.2 | 110.3 |
| 1963 | 15.5 | 110.8 | 19.9 | 12.7 | 8.1 | 106.8 | 104.8 | 111.0 | 105.0 |
| 1964 | 3.3 | 112.4 | 20.2 | 12.8 | 8.5 | 103.7 | 102.3 | 125.8 | 111.4 |
| 1965 | 1.3 | 109.7 | 18.1 | 13.2 | 5.5 | 96.6 | 105.9 | 112.0 | 100.4 |
| **CZECHOSLOVAKIA** | | | | | | | | | |
| 1963 | -11.2 | 99.9 | 19.0 | 12.6 | 6.8 | 85.5 | 89.3 | 98.3 | 82.3 |
| 1964 | 11.1 | 101.2 | 17.7 | 16.0 | 0.5 | 92.7 | 93.0 | 110.3 | 87.0 |
| 1965 | 7.5 | 102.1 | 16.9 | 15.0 | 1.0 | 99.8 | 89.4 | 109.3 | 97.7 |
| 1966 | 9.5 | 101.6 | 20.6 | 13.5 | 7.5 | 99.7 | 97.2 | 114.0 | 113.9 |
| 1967 | 3.0 | 101.2 | 20.8 | 12.7 | 8.9 | 94.1 | 98.5 | 99.5 | 99.3 |
| **BULGARIA** | | | | | | | | | |
| 1965 | 7.4 | 101.6 | 28.3 | 15.0 | 13.3 | 93.6 | 95.6 | 140.8 | 131.9 |
| 1966 | 19.6 | 106.2 | 34.3 | 16.1 | 17.8 | 103.1 | 106.6 | 171.0 | 172.5 |
| 1967 | 23.6 | 105.7 | 33.9 | 20.4 | 13.6 | 102.6 | 98.6 | 143.9 | 162.4 |
| 1968 | 9.0 | 105.8 | 32.2 | 18.9 | 13.4 | 107.6 | 106.5 | 135.0 | 140.0 |
| 1969 | 1.0 | 102.8 | 33.2 | 22.7 | 10.8 | 98.0 | 100.0 | 98.5 | 130.0 |
| **ROMANIA** | | | | | | | | | |
| 1965 | 9.0 | ... | ... | ... | ... | 87.3 | 91.3 | 131.5 | 111.7 |
| 1966 | 9.9 | ... | ... | ... | ... | 94.4 | 95.3 | 130.7 | 112.8 |
| 1967 | 16.6 | ... | ... | ... | ... | 95.5 | 93.0 | 165.0 | 147.8 |
| 1968 | 11.7 | ... | ... | ... | ... | 94.7 | 91.3 | 156.6 | 145.5 |
| 1969 | 6.6 | ... | ... | ... | ... | 91.5 | 106.0 | 147.9 | 135.1 |
| **G.D.R.** | | | | | | | | | |
| 1966 | 6.9 | 1.6 | 6.2 | 1.9 | 17.3 | 96.7 | 113.6 | 120.2 | 117.6 |
| 1967 | 9.3 | -0.8 | 1.0 | 10.1 | -23.3 | 92.1 | 100.3 | 109.5 | 103.9 |
| 1968 | 11.0 | -2.6 | -7.8 | 7.6 | -77.0 | 88.1 | 93.8 | 97.1 | 86.7 |
| 1969 | 16.0 | 3.4 | 12.5 | 12.8 | 8.0 | 98.5 | 106.7 | 105.4 | 87.2 |
| 1970 | 7.0 | 2.1 | 10.9 | -3.1 | 255.6 | 99.3 | 111.6 | 129.3 | 107.7 |
| 1971 | 1.3 | -1.4 | -5.4 | -6.4 | 3.2 | 90.4 | 99.3 | 128.4 | 107.8 |

94

| Year | GINV | NMPUT/PR | ACC/UT | FA/UT | STOCK/UT | M/XSOC | M/XUSSR | M/XOECD | M/XOECDC |
| --- | --- | --- | --- | --- | --- | --- | --- | --- | --- |
| | | | | (% change) | | | | | |
| **POLAND** | | | | | | | | | |
| 1970 | 4.0 | 100.4 | 35.8 | 26.9 | 10.4 | 109.1 | 107.0 | 92.4 | 85.8 |
| 1971 | 7.4 | 102.0 | 37.5 | 27.0 | 12.6 | 111.4 | 105.3 | 95.4 | 86.9 |
| 1972 | 23.0 | 103.8 | 40.3 | 30.4 | 11.6 | 104.2 | 87.4 | 121.1 | 106.8 |
| 1973 | 25.4 | 107.1 | 45.1 | 34.0 | 13.0 | 104.1 | 92.9 | 158.8 | 133.2 |
| 1974 | 22.3 | 108.6 | 48.5 | 37.1 | 13.3 | 100.5 | 105.3 | 176.6 | 146.7 |
| 1975 | 10.7 | 109.1 | 47.4 | 38.0 | 10.6 | 93.2 | 101.7 | 190.7 | 152.2 |
| 1976 | 1.0 | 108.8 | 45.5 | 35.3 | 11.6 | 98.8 | 110.7 | 192.4 | 135.2 |
| 1977 | 3.1 | 105.9 | 41.7 | 35.5 | 6.8 | 102.7 | 111.3 | 165.1 | 117.7 |
| 1978 | 2.1 | 103.4 | 40.6 | 33.9 | 7.4 | 101.0 | 95.8 | 147.6 | 116.0 |
| 1979 | -7.9 | 101.9 | 34.1 | 29.8 | 4.7 | 96.4 | 103.2 | 131.8 | 105.1 |

Labels: GINV      = Total gross investments
NMPUT/PR  = Ratio of NMP utilized vs. NMP produced (GDR: Percentage point difference between annual growth rates of respective variables)
ACC/UT    = Ratio of net accumulation vs. NMP used (GDR: Percentage point difference between annual growth rates of respective variables)
FA/UT     = Ratio of net fixed capital formation vs. NMP used (GDR: Percentage point difference between annual growth rates of respective variables)
STOCK/UT  = Ratio of stock building vs. NMP used (GDR: Percentage point difference between annual growth rates of respective variables)
M/XSOC    = Import coverage ratio in trade with soc. countries
M/XUSSR   = Import coverage ratio in trade with the USSR (Soviet mirror statistics, at current TR)
M/XOECD   = Import coverage ratio in trade with industrial market economies (in current national currency units)
M/XOECDC  = Import coverage ratio in trade with OECD countries. (OECD mirror statistics) SITC 0-9 at current US $

Source: ECE Common Data Base, derived from national or CMEA statistics; United Nations commodity trade data (COMTRADE) and Statistisches Bundesamt, Warenverkehr mit der Deutschen Demokratischen Republik und Berlin (Ost), Reihe 6, Wiesbaden.

SYMBOLS EMPLOYED:      ...      NOT AVAILABLE
                                NOT APPLICABLE
                        -       MAGNITUDE NOT ZERO, BUT LESS THAN HALF OF UNITY EMPLOYED
                        0       MAGNITUDE ZERO

available only in index form, possible tensions could be detected only in terms of growth rate differences (in percentage points). Now, these changes seem to be largely invariant to GINV fluctuations.

As already mentioned above, it is impossible to reconstruct the true balance-of-payments consequences of the investment cycle from published sources. The most that outside research can provide is a separate analysis of aggregate trade balances according to trading partners: trade with the socialist countries, with the Soviet Union, and with the OECD countries. This seems to be a justified simplification, since trade flows with the socialist countries other than the Soviet Union, as well as with the developing countries, are probably irrelevant from the point of view of the investment cycle.

In Bulgaria and Czechoslovakia, the reaction pattern of trade balances to the investment cycle was uniform for both types of trade [11]. As the pace of investments quickened, the trade balances deteriorated, but then they improved as soon as GINV rates started to fall. By contrast, only the western trade balance's deterioration moved cyclically in Poland and in Romania. Here, as well as in Bulgaria, the evidence is fairly robust: in peak years the value of total imports surpassed that of exports by 40-90 per cent. In the GDR, the trade position with the socialist countries proved to be slightly positively correlated with the cycle, while the trade balance with the western economies appears to behave anti-cyclically. No clear picture emerges in the Hungarian or Romanian case. In both countries trade with socialist partners resulted in growing deficits as domestic investment picked up. At the same time, however, both countries improved their trade positions vis-a-vis the Soviet Union [12].

Needless to say, the coincidence of the GINV cycle with changes in the trade balance does not prove that the former was the cause of the latter. An examination of the size of the increments of machinery purchases relative to the absolute increase in total imports can help to come closer to a conclusion. As regards the changes in imports from the socialist countries, it appears that only in two cases were machinery imports largely responsible for the deterioration of the trade balance. In other cases the increments in the SOCMACH variable (measured in terms of current dollar values) accounted for only 30-40 per cent of the rise in total imports. For machinery imports from non-socialist countries, the results were similar.

The findings of our examinations concerning the link between the GINV cycle and the role of imported machinery are summarised in Table 5.6. The emerging pattern suggests <u>that there was only a single case</u> (Romania) <u>where the cyclical movement of the machinery imports</u>

can be directly blamed for the deterioration in both types of trade balances. In two cases, the deterioration in the socialist trade balance can be largely, but in three cases only partly, explained by the cyclical fluctuation observed in machinery imports. In trade with the OECD countries, the tensions in the balance were also provoked in two cases by the sudden rise in machinery imports. In Romania this factor accounted for two thirds, in Bulgaria for more than half of the rise in total foreign purchases. In all the remaining cases, either the changes in the balances were independent from the GINV cycle, or their cyclical movements were largely attributable to other factors.

## 3. The role of the crop harvest

Among the several possible random factors that may have a major impact on the investment process, the agricultural crop harvest is the most obvious one. It will be recalled that in the periods under investigation, the size of the annual harvest was of considerable macro-economic importance in all the countries in the region and much more variable than the industry sector. Thus, the harvest not only had a major impact on NMP growth in the given year [13], but it also influenced the domestic food [14] and fodder supply - as well as the countries' export potential - in the given and in the following year. The size of the crop harvest is not known with satisfactory precision before the ninth month of the year. Not surprisingly, investments in the year in question are hardly influenced. But investment plans for the following year are usually elaborated just about this time. To set its likely influence in proportion, it is worth mentioning that the crop harvest's gross value in the periods under discussion was equivalent to 70-100 per cent of GINV in the four countries (GDR, Hungary, Poland and Romania) for which data are available at comparable prices for both aggregates. In these economies the total gross value of annual agricultural output was about 50-80 per cent above GINV levels.

As is shown in Table 5.7, wild fluctuations in the crop harvest were registered in a number of countries in the periods examined. But this fact does not necessarily imply straightforward,identical consequences in all the countries concerned. In Hungary, for example, the trade impact of the poor harvests in 1964 and 1965 is difficult to interpret. Agricultural exports to the socialist countries grew fast in 1964, while sales to the West (which were about the same size in volume terms) fell back. In the following year, when crop output actually fell by 7 per

97

Table 5.6
Machinery imports and deterioration of trade balances (a)

| | Socialist trade (b) | | Trade with OECD countries (c) | |
|---|---|---|---|---|
| | Trade balance cyclical | Increment of machinery import in % of increment of total import | Trade balance cyclical | Increment of machinery import in % of increment of total import |
| BULGARIA | + | 44 % | + | 57 % |
| CZECHOSL. | + | 55 % | + | 35 % |
| GDR | + | 37 % | - | . |
| HUNGARY | - | 33 % | - | . |
| POLAND | - | . | + | 41 % |
| ROMANIA | - | 61 % | + | 66 % |

Notes: (a) Measured between pre-cycle trough and the peak year of the cycle in terms of current dollar prices.
(b) On the basis of national statistics
(c) On the basis of OECD partner statistics.

Source: ECE Common Data Base, derived from national or CMEA statistics; United Nations commodity trade data (COMTRADE) and Statistisches Bundesamt, Warenverkehr mit der Deutschen Demokratischen Republik und Berlin (Ost), Reihe 6, Wiesbaden.

| SYMBOLS EMPLOYED: | ... | NOT AVAILABLE |
|---|---|---|
| | . | NOT APPLICABLE |
| | - | MAGNITUDE NOT ZERO, BUT LESS THAN HALF OF UNITY EMPLOYED |
| | 0 | MAGNITUDE ZERO |
| | + | SIGNIFICANT MAGNITUDE, BUT NOT QUANTIFIED |

## TABLE 5.7
### Total investments and variations in agriculture
### (Annual percentage change)

| | Year | GINV | CROP | ANIMAL | XSOC | MSOC | XOECD | MOECD |
|---|---|---|---|---|---|---|---|---|
| HUNGARY | 1961 | -1.1 | -6.3 | 5.6 | 22.0 | -0.5 | ... | ... |
| | 1962 | 10.0 | 6.1 | -0.0 | 8.4 | 20.8 | ... | ... |
| | 1963 | 15.5 | 8.3 | 0.9 | 4.0 | 3.4 | 27.3 | 38.5 |
| | 1964 | 3.3 | 0.8 | 9.9 | 18.8 | 4.8 | -6.5 | -36.0 |
| | 1965 | 1.3 | -7.0 | -3.3 | -1.0 | 24.3 | 21.1 | 14.2 |
| CZECHOSLOVAKIA | 1963 | -11.2 | 16.2 | -0.7 | 30.7 | 11.7 | 29.1 | -5.1 |
| | 1964 | 11.1 | -0.8 | 7.9 | -26.5 | -16.3 | -15.5 | 13.9 |
| | 1965 | 7.5 | -15.5 | 2.8 | 1.4 | 7.3 | 3.1 | 39.8 |
| | 1966 | 9.5 | 21.7 | 3.4 | -14.6 | 19.1 | -5.8 | 25.1 |
| | 1967 | 3.0 | 4.6 | 5.8 | 20.9 | 4.4 | 13.9 | -33.1 |
| BULGARIA | 1965 | .4 | -1.5 | 8.3 | 21.4 | -37.3 | 41.5 | 49.3 |
| | 1966 | 19.6 | 19.0 | 5.8 | 7.0 | 42.4 | 27.9 | 26.9 |
| | 1967 | 23.6 | 1.8 | 6.9 | 19.6 | 9.8 | -4.4 | -38.1 |
| | 1968 | 9.0 | -10.3 | -1.1 | 9.1 | 36.8 | -4.6 | 113.1 |
| | 1969 | 1.0 | 6.8 | -1.6 | 12.9 | -1.5 | -7.4 | -40.6 |
| ROMANIA | 1965 | 9.0 | 6.7 | 4.7 | 8.6 | -43.4 | 20.6 | 9.2 |
| | 1966 | 9.9 | 16.1 | 12.1 | -3.5 | 22.0 | -3.9 | -2.5 |
| | 1967 | 16.6 | -2.1 | 7.7 | 2.8 | 50.6 | 74.5 | 67.3 |
| | 1968 | 11.7 | -3.4 | -2.9 | 0.2 | -3.4 | -28.6 | -28.6 |
| | 1969 | 6.6 | 5.3 | -0.5 | -1.4 | 7.8 | 15.8 | 3.7 |
| G.D.R. | 1966 | 6.9 | 1.8 | 5.1 | 3.8 | 17.9 | 73.8 | -15.2 |
| | 1967 | 9.3 | 12.6 | 1.4 | 42.6 | 19.7 | 20.0 | -29.3 |
| | 1968 | 11.0 | -1.9 | 4.2 | -4.0 | -13.2 | -27.1 | -29.2 |
| | 1969 | 16.0 | -16.1 | -0.7 | 11.7 | 19.9 | 26.7 | 34.2 |
| | 1970 | 7.0 | 10.5 | -0.0 | 138.2 | 21.1 | -0.8 | -11.7 |
| | 1971 | 1.3 | -5.9 | 4.0 | -0.2 | -5.3 | 2.2 | 18.5 |
| POLAND | 1970 | 4.0 | 4.3 | -1.1 | 8.3 | -14.4 | 11.4 | 45.5 |
| | 1971 | 7.4 | 1.1 | 6.6 | -18.8 | 53.2 | 4.1 | 11.3 |
| | 1972 | 23.0 | 7.8 | 9.0 | 59.0 | -26.7 | 26.0 | 21.2 |
| | 1973 | 25.4 | 6.5 | 8.2 | -8.5 | -12.4 | 40.7 | 28.7 |
| | 1974 | 22.3 | -0.7 | 4.2 | 70.8 | 52.8 | -9.6 | 2.4 |
| | 1975 | 10.7 | -3.0 | -1.0 | -12.0 | -10.8 | -8.9 | 26.4 |
| | 1976 | 1.0 | 5.0 | -8.7 | -26.8 | -37.9 | 20.4 | 37.0 |
| | 1977 | 3.1 | -7.2 | 13.7 | -6.1 | 44.7 | 4.3 | -23.3 |
| | 1978 | 2.1 | 5.4 | 2.6 | 1.2 | -6.4 | 14.3 | 65.0 |
| | 1979 | -7.9 | -3.7 | 1.3 | 9.0 | -7.6 | 13.3 | 24.1 |

Labels:
GINV      = Total gross investments
CROP      = Crop output
ANIMAL  = Livestock output
XSOC      = Exports of raw materials for food industry, livestocks and processed food products
                    into socialist countries.
MSOC      = Imports of raw materials for food industry, livestocks and processed food products
                    from socialist countries.
XOECD   = Exports of food, beverages and tobacco to OECD countries. SITC 0-1 at current US $
MOECD  = Imports of food, beverages and tobacco from OECD countries. SITC 0-1 at current US $

Source: ECE Common Data Base, derived from national or CMEA statistics; United Nations commodity trade data (COMTRADE) and Statistisches Bundesamt, Warenverkehr mit der Deutschen Demokratischen Republik und Berlin (Ost), Reihe 6, Wiesbaden.

SYMBOLS EMPLOYED:  ... NOT AVAILABLE; . NOT APPLICABLE ; - MAGNITUDE NOT ZERO, BUT LESS THAN HALF OF UNITY EMPLOYED; 0  MAGNITUDE ZERO cent only, exports to the socialist countries suffered, while exports to the west grew by more than 20 per cent. (Partly as a consequence of these efforts, but also for other reasons, by 1965 the country almost balanced its trade with the OECD countries, while according to the OECD partner statistics it even attained a small surplus in 1966.) The domestic impact of the 1965 harvest was quite brutal: the growth rate of NMP produced was virtually zero, much lower than in any other year in the historically long 1957-1978 period.

The years 1964-1965 were also difficult in Czechoslovakia. After a year of stagnation, the 1965 crop harvest fell by more than 15 per cent - an unprecedented magnitude in the entire post-war history of the country. Accordingly, NMP growth was also adversely affected (1964: 0.6%; 1965: 3.4%). Agricultural exports to the OECD countries were also hit, but given their small weight in currency earnings (around 14 per cent), these consequences were not very severe. In trade with the socialist countries, however, the changes in the following year were already noteworthy. The growth dynamic of machinery imports was almost halted, while food imports - representing about one third of all socialist imports - grew by nearly 20 per cent.

In Bulgaria, the bad harvests in 1967 and 1968 were presumably one of the major reasons behind the fall in agricultural exports to the OECD countries. By 1968, the amount of total machinery import (SITC 7) originating from this area effectively fell below the level of the country's food exports (SITC 0-1). NMP growth also reacted sensitively. After two years of high rates, close to 10 per cent on average, the 17 per cent fall in net agricultural output pulled down the 1968 NMP growth rate to 6 per cent.

The peak year of the GDR's investment cycle, 1969, coincided with a very bad harvest. Crop output fell by more than 16 per cent. (In fact this was the second worst year in the country's history, after the harvest shortfall of more than 27 per cent, recorded in 1961.) But given the small contribution of the agricultural sector to NMP, the aggregate output performance was not severely affected. Despite the small harvest, the level of western food exports was considerably increased in that year and it was then maintained over the next two years. The motives behind this decision are not difficult to see: in good years - even for the relatively industrialised GDR economy - food export accounted for more than 20 per cent of total export incomes originating from western trade [15]. Poland and Romania were fortunate enough, not to be hit by any major harvest shortfall during the period analysed here. In conclusion, it can be said that in three cases out of four the sudden shortfall of the agricultural crop harvest imposed a major constraint on the economies. Of course, it would go beyond the confines of this paper to investigate the full consequences of harvest failures. But it is the author's opinion that a more detailed investigation could reveal important direct links between the poor harvest and restrictive investment policies in the following year in other countries and other periods, too.

## 4. Summary and conclusions

The statistical account presented above indicates a number of country and time-specific differences among the cycles, although only a small sample was analysed. This fact in itself is an obvious warning against precipitate generalisations concerning the 'typical' course of east European investment cycles. Nonetheless, a few common features - valid for the majority of the cases investigated above - remain. Taking as a starting point a year when GINV expands very slowly or even contracts, and assuming that no major external shock or internal political crisis shakes the economy in the next 3-4 years, the following scenario seems to be rather typical.

As the investment process quickens, non-residential construction activity and machinery imports also start to to grow at accelerated rates. So far, this is in line with received wisdom. Surprisingly, however, it is found that personal consumption goes hand in hand with the investment cycle. But the dynamic impetus originating from rapid increases in investment does not lead to sustainable investment-led growth. Industrial output often remains invariant to changes in GINV. There is a great probability that within a five-year period one or two bad crop harvests occur. It seems that a significant shortfall in crop output alone leads to a noticeable curtailment of investment. For several reasons - i.e. not only because of the increased machinery import - the trade balance soon begins to deteriorate. There is no general rule as to which regional balance goes into deficit. In some cases the burden falls on the socialist, in other cases on the western trade balance. It is therefore understandable that after 2-3 years [16] the immediate curtailment of investment growth appears to be the quickest and least painful remedy to restore the trade balance. Nonetheless, the easing of this tension typically does not come about within one or two years.

**Notes**

[1]   Revised version of a paper presented at the Conference on 'Fluctuations and Cycles in Socialist Economies' held at the University of Padua (March 13-14, 1987). The author is with the General Economic Analysis Division of the <u>United Nations Economic Commission for Europe in Geneva</u>. The views presented here are his own and do not reflect in any way an expression of opinion on the part of the ECE.

[2]   These behavioural issues were discussed at great length on a country-by-country basis in Bauer's book. (See: Bauer, T.: *Tervgazdasag, beruhazas, ciklusok* (Planning, investment, cycles), Kozgazdasagi es Jogi Konyvkiado, Budapest, 1981.

[3]   The views of the author on these subjects were presented in a paper entitled 'La synchronisation des fluctuation de l'investissement en Europe de l'Est, 1950-1985', in Chavance, B. (ed.), *Régulation, cycles et crises dans les économies socialistes*, Editions de l'Ecole des Hautes Etudes en Sciences Sociales, Paris, 1987.

[4]   But we deliberately deviated from this approach, when trade balances were examined. Here current price data were always used in order to give a better illustration of the difficulties that the countries' economic decision makers  actually faced.

[5]   Another consideration also supported this approach. As is well known, until the late 1950s, the economic policies of the East European countries were - to a large extent - subordinated to the capricious changes in the policy stance of the Soviet Union. Therefore, this period does not seem to be appropriate for a cross-country analysis, since the overall outcome would be too predetermined by the changes in the Soviet Union

[6]   The years in brackets indicate the timing of the cycle in a trough-peak-trough scheme. For the sake of precision, it should be noted that the 1961-1963-1965 cycle in Hungary had a slightly smaller peak than the second omitted one. In many respects these two cycles were equally regular, closely resembling a bell-shape curve. Thus here the choice was somewhat accidental. On the other hand, the year 1968 coincided with the start of the New Economic Mechanism, and this fact in itself spoke in favour of the selected earlier cycle.The striking time regularity of the Hungarian investment cycles, in contrast to the apparently more haphazard fluctuations observed in the other East European countries is the

subject of A.K. Soós's paper ('Regular Investment Cycles or Irregular Investment Fluctuations under Central Planning'), presented at this conference

[7]   On a closer inspection of the complete EMPC time series, however, it cannot be excluded, that we are greatly misled by the apparent impact of an inconsequently implemented change in statistical classification. Therefore, the 13.1 per cent annual rise of EMPC in 1965 is a rather improbable magnitude, though nearly similar rates were recorded in 1959 (11.3 %) and even later in 1969 (8.8%).

[8]   This seems to confirm our doubts concerning the reliability of the 1965 EMPC figure for Hungary

[9]   The long term specificities of these imports were described in great detail in a recent ECE Secretariat study (See: 'Eastern Imports of Machinery and Equipment, 1960-1985', United Nations Economic Commission for Europe, *Economic Bulletin for Europe*, vol. 38, No.4. 1987, chapter 3.)

[10]  At this point, it is necessary to note that our analysis was carried out using time series, expressed in terms of the currently used constant price level of the country in question. Thus in this case 1981 prices were applied for Hungary. In fact, in terms of current prices, this ratio stood only at 103.3 in 1964. Even if 1968 constant prices were used the NMPUT/PR ratio is no more than 103.5. Here we face a practically insurmountable difficulty for any time series analysis. The construction of a useful data base requires the creation of time series consisting of absolute figures (rather than indices, or growth rates), but after repeated repricing of the time series, the relative proportions may change quite drastically, due to huge shifts in relative prices.

[11]  Mirror data for trade with the West also corroborate this finding.

[12]  In the remaining cases the countries' positions vis-a-vis the Soviet Union and the countries of the socialist community as a whole behaved similarly. The two above mentioned cases are somewhat surprising, since in the middle of the 1960s the Soviet Union was the most important supplier of machinery, imported by socialist countries from other socialist countries (around 30 per cent).

[13]  In 1965, according to contemporary CMEA statistics the net contribution of agriculture to NMP varied between 12.0 per cent (Czechoslovakia) and 32.5 per cent (Bulgaria).

[14]  In the second part of the 1960s food accounted for about 50 per cent of total retail trade in these countries.

[15] The surge of food export to the socialist countries was spectacular in percentage terms, but it was nonetheless a negligible development, given the small absolute size of the trade flow.

[16] The exceptional length of the full investment cycle in Poland (1970-1979) can only be explained by two factors. First the country was lucky with the weather and no major harvest shortfalls occurred. (But this happened in 1980: crop output plunged by more than 15 per cent, causing additional hardships to the conflict ridden Polish economy.) Secondly, in the 1970s Eastern Europe was given access to sizeable foreign credits - a possibility which simply did not exist for other countries in the earlier periods.

# 6 Cyclical fluctuations in centrally planned economies: some cross-country considerations

BARRY W. ICKES

## Introduction

That Centrally Planned Economies (CPE's) are subject to cyclical fluctuations has become an accepted fact in recent years [1]. This has led to much theorising about the causes of cycles in these economies. But there has been less attention devoted towards a comparative study of cycles in CPE's (Tyson 1983 and Mihalyi 1986 are exceptions). Most studies have instead focused on the experiences of particular countries. This makes it difficult to distinguish the extent to which the observed phenomena are the result of policy as opposed to some common systemic element.

The purpose of this paper is to begin to redress this shortcoming. We examine the cyclical experiences of the six East European CPE's (Bulgaria, Czechoslovakia, German Democratic Republic, Hungary, Poland, and Romania) and the Soviet Union. Our primary focus is on the extent to which these economies share a common cyclical experience. We will also explore the implications of the observed economic time series for theorising about the nature and causes of these cyclical fluctuations.

# 1.

Cycles are a more complex phenomenon than economic instability. To identify the latter we look at such indices as the variance of the growth rate of output [2]. To identify a cycle we also seek evidence that the fluctuations follow a pattern. In particular, we expect adjacent periods to share common features. A series of random fluctuations certainly indicates instability. But a cycle implies more; it implies a patterned sort of instability. This does not necessarily imply that the fluctuations must be regular or periodic (Ickes 1986). Experience in market economies suggests that cycles are quite irregular. But we would expect to observe significant serial correlations if a time series is cyclical.

The very notion of a cycle implies variation around something. The question is around what? The classical NBER approach (Burns and Mitchell 1946, 39) was to assume that 'something' to be a given level. Thus expansions are identified by positive growth rates and downturns by negative growth rates. This approach proved useful to those who wished to deny the existence of any cycles in CPE's. Since CPE growth rates were consistently nonnegative until the late 70's, it could be argued that the socialist economies did not exhibit cycles. To assume that the fluctuations must be around a flat trend is, however, an arbitrary and quite misleading assumption. If economies are growing rapidly, a cyclical downturn need not cause the rate of growth to turn negative. By focusing on a mean of zero, analysts arbitrarily exclude from view items of interest.

The response of many analysts is to estimate a trend and then identify the cyclical fluctuations as the residuals. The trend is estimated by regressing the log of output (NMP) on time (and possibly time squared to account for the slowing of growth). This is common practice in standard macroeconomics and in modern business cycle research (Klein and Moore 1985). This seems straightforward, since economists are used to thinking about cycles as deviations from an equilibrium growth path. As we shall see below (in section 5, this procedure raises some important questions. At the moment, however, we follow accepted practice.

In Table 6.1 we report the results for the 'Six' and for the USSR. The data is Net Material Product, and the period is from 1960-1984. In Table 6.2 we report the results for investment. The results are not surprising. The negative coefficients on time squared indicates the slowing of growth over the period. The very low Durbin-Watson statistics suggests the presence of serial correlation. This is verified in Table 6.3 where the autocorrelations are presented for the residuals in the equations for output and investment. Notice that they are significant at lag one, and then peter out. This is consistent with the hypothesis that these economies experienced cyclical fluctuations during this period.

The results in Tables 6.1 and 6.2 look quite similar. It is not too surprising that investment and net material product have similar time series properties. It is important to note, however, that for each country (with the exception of Romania for which there is no reliable series on investment) investment is more volatile than output. This is indicated in Table 6.4 which reports the coefficient of variation of the growth rate of investment and output for each country. Table 6.4 indicates that the various CPE's differ in volatility, but in each case the series for investment is significantly more volatile than output. This suggests that consumption is more stable than investment, though we lack a series with which to test this. If this inference is proper, it suggests that it may be incorrect to assume that planners in CPE's treat consumption as a buffer. Indeed, as we shall see below, it may make more sense to view planners as trying to maintain consumption, with investment bearing most of the brunt of shocks.

Let us, for now, treat the residuals in the above equations as cyclical fluctuations around a deterministic trend. It will be interesting to see how these fluctuations in the various economies coincide. In Tables 6.5 and 6.6 we present the correlations of the residuals across countries. The results are quite interesting. Focusing on Table 6.5 we observe a very strong coincidence in the timing of these fluctuations [3]. Notice that among the 'Six' the lowest correlation is .659, and all but one of the correlations in the table is above .500. These results (and the associated ones for investment in Table 6.6) are surprising. Most of the literature on cycles in CPE's has focused on domestic explanations [4]. Yet it is difficult to see how purely domestic factors would cause such temporal coincidence. One possible explanation - the coincidence of Five Year Plans - is rejected on the basis of a test that included dummy variables for the initial year of the (coincident) plans. The coefficients were all insignificant. Visual inspection of the plot of the residuals above indicates that the cycles bear no relationship to the FYP's.

The common variation in output is mirrored (but to a lesser extent) in the results for investment. This is not surprising given the strong correlation between the investment cycle and the output cycle (Table 6.7). That is, the results in Table 6.7 - where a strong relationship between investment and output - is not of itself surprising. Economists have for a long time suggested that the two series are related. But the usual direction of causality has been treated as from investment to output. Hence the development of theories of the investment cycle, which focus on problems in the process of investment planning as the source of cycles (Bauer 1978, Ickes 1986). The common variation, however, suggests that the causation may go the other way. Suppose investment is related to changes in (expected) output in an accelerator-like fashion. Then if the cycles in output were caused by a common external disturbance, we would expect to observe common fluctuations in investment. The common view - investment » output, due to say the vagaries of planners in individual CPE's - on the other hand, would seem to imply cycles that are not temporally coincident (but see below, section 5).

The data in Tables 6.1-6.7 present us with some outlines of the nature of cyclical fluctuations in CPE's. Of interest are the common features across countries. In each of the countries the cycle in output is correlated with a cycle in investment. These cycles tend to have low frequencies. In each of the countries investment is more volatile than output. Most interesting of all, the cycles in the various East European CPE's tend to coincide. These 'stylised facts' suggest that there may be a systemic aspect to these cycles. Since the patterns are similar across countries it suggests that purely (domestic) political explanations will not wash. The common variations seems to suggest that explanations of the cycle that focus only on the domestic economy may be fundamentally inadequate. For if their cause is purely domestic, why the coincident timing? Indeed the common variation is interesting in and of itself, as we would not expect planned economies to share common cyclical behaviour.


2.


The natural place to search for an explanation of the common variation in East European performance is trade behaviour. One would expect that countries which trade with one another might transmit their economic maladies to each other. When a country experiences an economic boom income is high resulting in increased imports which transmit the prosperity to the country's trading partners. In a slump a country's imports decline, and again the effects of the slump are transmitted through changes in trade flows. One might search for the cause of the common variation in the trade behaviour of economically interdependent economies.

Such a conjecture seems valid when one looks at market economies. In Table 6.8 we show the cross-country correlations for a sample of OECD countries. The countries in the sample are major trading part-

## Table 6.1
## Net material product, 1960-1984

|  | T | $T_2$ | $R^2$ | DW | $\rho$ |
|---|---|---|---|---|---|
| Bulgaria | .092 (34.63) | -.001 (- 8.34) | .998 | .529 | .512 |
| Czechoslovakia | .058 (9.51) | -.0005 (- 2.22) | .972 | .263 | .794 |
| GDR | .048 (22.37) | - .00008 (- 1.058) | .997 | .386 | .646 |
| Poland | .110 (9.29) | -.002 (-5.23) | .938 | .259 | .836 |
| Hungary | .071 (15.27) | -.0008 (-4.88) | .988 | .396 | .728 |
| USSR | .084 (39.14) | -.0016 (-13.24) | .998 | .748 | .514 |
| Romania | .105 (17.02) | -.0009 (- 4.01) | .993 | .240 | .822 |

Source: Vienna Institute for Comparative Economic Studies

Equation form : $\text{Log}(NMP_t) = \beta_0 + \beta_1 T + \cdot\beta_2 T^2 + \varepsilon$


## Table 6.2
## Investment, 1960-1984

|  | T | $T_2$ | $R^2$ | DW | $\rho$ |
|---|---|---|---|---|---|
| Bulgaria | .139 (19.32) | -.002 (-7.99) | .990 | 1.29 | .229 |
| Czechoslovakia | .076 (7.02) | - .0009 (- 2.35) | .947 | .343 | .744 |
| GDR | .106 (14.72) | -.002 (- 7.35) | .979 | .430 | .620 |
| Poland | .169 (6.85) | -.004 (-4.37) | .862 | .245 | .843 |
| Hungary | .120 (12.94) | -.003 (- 7.43) | .966 | .762 | .494 |
| USSR | .087 (25.18) | -.001 (- 8.50) | .995 | .569 | .585 |

Source: Vienna Institute for Comparative Economic Studies

Equation form: $\text{Log}(I_t) = \beta_0 + \beta_1 T + \beta_2 T^2 + \varepsilon$

## Table 6.3
### Autocorrelations (on residuals)

#### NMP

|       |   | Bulgaria | Czech. | GDR | Hungary | Poland | Romania | USSR |
|-------|---|----------|--------|-----|---------|--------|---------|------|
| Lag | 1 | .523 | .794 | .646 | .728 | .836 | .827 | .513 |
|     | 2 | .175 | .422 | .340 | .483 | .508· | .509 | .181 |
|     | 3 | .008 | .055 | .117 | .252 | .165 | .193 | -.047 |
|     | 4 | -.149 | -.175 | -.027 | -.047 | -.131 | -.102 | -.213 |
|     | 5 | -.238 | -.274 | -.185 | -.319 | -.344 | -.325 | -.295 |

#### Investment

|       |   | Bulgaria | Czech. | GDR | Hungary | Poland | USSR |
|-------|---|----------|--------|-----|---------|--------|------|
| Lag | 1 | .229 | .744 | .619 | .494 | .843 | .584 |
|     | 2 | -.123 | .366 | .223 | .119 | .538 | .289 |
|     | 3 | -.303 | .063 | -.068 | .011 | .189 | .083 |
|     | 4 | -.391 | -.046 | -.158 | -.150 | -.104 | -.037 |
|     | 5 | -.277 | -.178 | -.276 | -.489 | -.329 | -.178 |

Source: Vienna Institute for Comparative Economic Studies

## Table 6.4
### Coefficient of variation of growth rate
### in %

|                | NMP | I |
|----------------|--------|--------|
| Bulgaria | 28.44 | 99.18 |
| Czechoslovakia | 67.57 | 124.07 |
| GDR | 25.16 | 96.75 |
| Hungary | 60.78 | 166.81 |
| Poland | 125.06 | 192.13 |
| Romania | 38.02 | N.A. |
| USSR | 37.18 | 45.29 |

$$\frac{Y_t}{Y_{t-1}} - 1 = \bar{g} \qquad CV = \frac{\sigma_g}{\bar{g}}$$

Source: Vienna Institute for Comparative Economic Studies

Table 6.5
Correlations of residuals (NMP)

| | Bulgaria | Czech. | GDR | Hungary | Poland | Romania | USSR |
|---|---|---|---|---|---|---|---|
| Bulgaria | 1.0 | .807 | .859 | .771 | .659 | .692 | .712 |
| Czech. | | 1.0 | .849 | .867 | .757 | .682 | .764 |
| GDR | | | 1.0 | .775 | .734 | .668 | .816 |
| Hungary | | | | 1.0 | .838 | .804 | .584 |
| Poland | | | | | 1.0 | .941 | .552 |
| Romania | | | | | | 1.0 | .431 |
| USSR | | | | | | | 1.0 |

Source: Table 6.1

Table 6.6
Correlations across countries (Investment)

| | Bulgaria | Czech. | GDR | Hungary | Poland | USSR |
|---|---|---|---|---|---|---|
| Bulgaria | 1.0 | .181 | .338 | .385 | .076 | .354 |
| Czech. | | 1.0 | .852 | .670 | .851 | .812 |
| GDR | | | 1.0 | .759 | .598 | .714 |
| Hungary | | | | 1.0 | .577 | .655 |
| Poland | | | | | 1.0 | .745 |
| USSR | | | | | | 1.0 |

Source: Table 6.2

Table 6.7
Correlation between NMP residuals and Investment residuals

| | |
|---|---|
| Bulgaria | .511 |
| Czechoslovakia | .937 |
| GDR | .850 |
| Hungary | .768 |
| Poland | .980 |
| USSR | .829 |

Source: Vienna Institute for Comparative Economic Studies

## Table 6.8
### Correlations of residuals across countries:
### selected market economies 1955-80

|         | U.K.  | France | Germany | Italy | U.S.  | Japan |
|---------|-------|--------|---------|-------|-------|-------|
| U.K.    | 1.000 | .692   | .646    | .471  | .693  | .619  |
| France  |       | 1.000  | .726    | .658  | .428  | .779  |
| Germany |       |        | 1.000   | .360  | .574  | .637  |
| Italy   |       |        |         | 1.000 | .295  | .759  |
| U.S.    |       |        |         |       | 1.000 | .527  |
| Japan   |       |        |         |       |       | 1.000 |

Source:  Vienna Institute for Comparative Economic Studies

ners. The correlations in the table seem to indicate the same level of common variation as in Tables 6.5 and 6.6.   Of course the countries in Table 6.8 are *market economies*. Trade in these economies is not the outcome of some central planning process. Rather trade is the result of the autonomous activities of individual agents and organisations (some state-owned but not centrally planned). The question to be answered is whether the conjecture will stand when we move to the CPE's.

There are two factors which suggest that trade may provide the link. First of all, these countries trade a good deal with each other. The share of each country's trade that remained within the bloc has been consistently over one half [5]. Like any customs union we would expect the existence of the CMEA to result in greater trade among its members (i.e., more than might be expected given comparative advantage and geography). And we know that the CMEA countries trade much more with each other today than they did prior to the Second World War. Whether this is the result of trade creation (through lower tariff barriers) or trade diversion (the more likely case) is not crucial for the moment. What is important is that the process of trade within CMEA might be expected to result in the kind of common variation we in fact observe. The East European 'common market' might act to integrate the various economies. This can happen in two ways. To the extent that the CMEA succeeds in developing joint planning (both current and investment), common performance would be expected. This would result in integration of the various economies.The second way involves increasing the flow of trade within the bloc.

Before we conclude that the patterns of trade and the existence of the CMEA is responsible for the common variation, it will be useful to examine the nature of trade in CPE's. The fact that trade is an outcome of the planning process implies that the autonomous mechanisms which are responsible for market economy integration will be absent.

There are several factors to note about the trade behaviour of CPE's [6]. First of all, CPE's are relatively autarchic. The ratio of trade to GNP in CPE's is significantly smaller for comparable levels of development, to that in market economies [7]. This is no doubt partly a reflection of the Stalinist legacy. But it is also a logical outcome to the institutions of the CPE's (which share the Stalinist heritage).

The most basic characteristic of trade in CPE's is the role of the foreign trade ministry (*FTM*) [8]. Enterprises do not decide to export a product because a higher price can be obtained abroad. Nor will it necessarily import a product that sells for less than the domestic price in world markets. Trade decisions are instead made by the FTM. The FTM decides what to trade based on the priorities given in the plan. Trade is thus viewed as an adjunct to the planning process, rather than an integral part of it. This causes Soviet-type economies (STE's) to take an 'antimercantilist view' (to use Holzman's felicitous phrase). Trade is conducted primarily to procure inputs that are too costly to produce domestically, and to fill in any imbalances in the plan. Exports are viewed as lost resources; they are the price that must be paid to obtain imports. They are not seen as an end but a means (which goes to show that one can learn some positive lessons from STE's). A STE does not export what it can. It rather exports what it can get away with to obtain the imports it desires.

Since the FTM stands between the domestic producers and the external market, the former have little incentive to produce goods that will be desired abroad. To the domestic producer it matters little who the purchaser will be. As long as the domestic economy continues to be a seller's market the producers find little trouble finding buyers. The problem of selling the exports falls to the FTM not the producing enterprise. But the FTM is also not concerned with the profit on any individual sale. Its concern is rather with being able to sell enough exports to fulfill its import plan.

The immediate consequence of the FTM is that the domestic economy in a CPE is insulated, to a large degree, from the effects of external shocks. Since the FTM purchases from enterprises at domestic prices there is no feedback from the world market to the structure of domestic prices. This price separation (the 'Preisausgleich') allows the STE to prevent internal prices from following movements in world prices. This is, of course, a two-edged sword. It is a benefit for a small country whose trading partners are suffering inflation. But it also pre-

113

vents relative price information from being transmitted to producers. For our purposes, however, the important point is that the FTM allows the STE to avoid the multiplier effects from trade shocks. No institutional device can prevent a deterioration in the terms of trade. But the STE is not subject to fluctuations in aggregate demand which can result from external shocks [9].

The key point is that changes in the external environment do not lead to *autonomous* movements in the domestic economy. The purpose of the FTM is precisely to insulate the domestic economy against these external influences. Otherwise the planning system could become unhinged. The effects are sometimes perverse to western eyes. Suppose that the terms of trade turn against the STE. One might expect exports to fall in such circumstances. But the STE has a target level of imports, the decline in the terms of trade might result in an increase in exports to pay for them. The crucial point, however, is that the response will be a *planning* decision. The impact on the domestic economy will depend on how the planners react.

Given the role of the planners in conducting trade one might expect the trade behaviour of CPE's to be *more* stable than in the West. The 'autarchy hypothesis' (Pryor 1968) suggests that given the smaller volume of trade, marginal units of trade should be more important to the CPE. Thus it is argued that, 'the foreign trade of these nations would be conducted in such a manner as to dampen 'natural' cyclical activity, so that the volume of trade would show more stability than in West Europe' (Pryor 1968, p. 162). But we know (Staller, 1964) that CPE's display as much or more instability than do western economies. This suggests that trade might be more unstable in the CPE's, to offset their 'natural' instability. And this is in fact what Staller (1967) found. Staller studied trade behaviour with respect to CMEA and OECD countries, and found that the former showed a more unstable pattern than the latter (or the U.S. for that matter, 1967, p. 881) [10].

What is not immediately apparent from Staller's data is the direction of causation. Is the instability in trade causing domestic instability (as the trade-based explanation of the common variation would suggest) or is it the other way around? This is a difficult question. It would be nice to perform a causality test (à la Granger-Sims), but unfortunately we do not (as yet) have adequate data for the task. We can, however, offer the suggestion that it is unlikely that the effect runs from trade to the domestic economy *via demand induced processes* (in the Keynesian tradition). It is extremely unlikely that the planners determine the level of intensity of domestic economic activity based on trade flows [11]. Most informed opinion argues that it is the imbalances in the domestic

114

economy, and what Rosefielde (1974) calls 'fundamental comparative advantage', which determines what the CPE wishes to trade. If trade instability does turn out to be 'causally prior' to domestic instability the process is most likely through supply shocks.

The insulation of the domestic economy in CPE's is furthered by the inconvertible character of their currencies. One is used to a currency being inconvertible if its exchange rate is overvalued. Here the problem is an incorrect relative price. The inconvertibility problems (it is not really a problem from the planners view) of STE's are wholly different. Inconvertibility in STE's results not from relative prices but from the planning system. If the planners determine interindustry flows through a system of plans, foreigners cannot be allowed to purchase what they want. If foreign holders of currency were allowed to purchase whatever they would like it would upset the plan [12]. Instead foreigners are allowed to purchase what the planners set aside for exports. Since CMEA currencies cannot be readily turned into commodities there is no inducement for foreigners to hold these currencies. Thus there is no way in which shifts in the foreign demand for these currencies can affect the economy; there is no foreign demand.

What of the role of the CMEA? The essential point is that the CMEA has not succeeded in producing a common market. Goods (let alone services) do not flow easily across borders. Indeed the CMEA has been hard pressed to find a way to end the process of bilateral trade among its members. Why does this trading group still persist in bilateral trade? The answer goes some way in explaining the perversities of trade in CPE's. Notice that if the CMEA acted as a customs union engaging in multilateral trade, we might expect to find a channel for the transmission of shocks across borders. The fact that such trade does not occur, [13] is not out of lack of effort. To further the prospects for multilateral trade among CMEA countries a clearing bank was created (International Bank for Economic Cooperation, or IBEC) in 1964, along with a common currency (the transferable ruble) for intra-bloc trade. But this has evidently gone for naught.

The idea behind the transferable ruble was to overcome the inconvertibility of bloc currencies through a system of settling accounts. Member countries would hold accounts with IBEC, and would be credited when exports were made and debited for imports. The idea was that accounts would be balanced over some period of time. In particular, the system was designed to avoid the need for members to balance their trade with each partner. Under the clearing house arrangement a Bulgarian deficit with Romania could be balanced by a Romanian deficit with Czechoslovakia and a Czech deficit with Bulgaria. If such a system could be made to work intra-bloc trade would become much less costly, resulting in greater exploitation of the gains from trade. But the system did not work as planned. The crux of the problem was the requirement that accounts in transferable rubles balance at the end of the year. Credit operations would be included as balancing items so that a strict balance did not have to be achieved each year. But this offered a large incentive for each member to try to generate a surplus within the bloc. A deficit would result in a loss of foreign exchange, while a surplus would earn some. By running a surplus within the bloc members could earn hard currency by trading within the CMEA! Of course the bloc as a whole cannot run a surplus with itself. But as each member tries, the trade of the bloc shrinks.

This problem is exacerbated by the 'pricing problem'. CPE's set prices on the basis of domestic average costs (often excluding high cost firms in the calculation!). If the CMEA is a 'high cost, low variety, low quality region' (Holzman 1979, p. 78), then this will result in a redirection of trade. Suppose intra-bloc trade is conducted at some average of domestic prices. Then prices within the bloc would be higher (when adjusted for quality) than world prices for the same products. Members would, under these circumstances prefer to export to the bloc and import from the rest of the world. Of course as it stands intra-bloc prices are based on averages of world market prices. But the same principles apply. To sell goods for which quality is important the CPE has to discount the price to sell in world markets [14]. These types of goods, especially machinery which accounts for an especially large share of bloc trade - 40% for 1960-64, 55% for 1970-74 (Marer and Montias 1980, p. 15) - get redirected to the bloc. Goods of rather homogeneous quality (e.g., agricultural goods or coal) can be sold in the West at world prices. These goods are then 'hard goods;' they enable the seller to earn hard currency. Soft goods then get sold within the bloc. But each member knows that the goods sold in the bloc are of inferior quality. Consequently members try to limit their purchases from within the bloc, exacerbating the drive to earn surpluses.

Under such circumstances the members of the bloc try to be careful about what they sell to each other. Bilateral balancing remains the norm. Members try to balance their trade with each partner to avoid settling a deficit with hard currency. The transferable ruble remains a unit of account, but is little else. And trade within the bloc reverts to a planned activity with minimal effect on CMEA integration.

There is a fundamental difference in the nature of integration, via customs unions, in the East and West. In the West, integration is basically promoted by reducing state intervention. Then trade will lead to integration via optimising agents exploiting comparative advantage. In the East, however, integration requires the intervention of the state. A CPE operates on the basis of central instructions. Thus to integrate CPE's requires integrating the central planners. Only if countries are willing to subordinate their plans to a supranational body can the bloc integrate. But this is something that has so far been politically infeasible [15]. And thus economic integration, despite much talk and effort, has proceeded very little.

We should finally note the importance of the sellers' market. Given the conditions of chronic excess demand in the production sector in CPE's, [16] an export surplus would not be able to generate (demand side) multiplier effects on income even if the FTM were abolished. Since resources are in short supply an export surplus does not represent an addition to demand, but rather a replacement of domestic uses by foreign ones. It is an import surplus than can have positive real output effects in the CPE. An excess of imports over exports can result in relief of bottlenecks that constrain production (Ickes, 1984). But the imports most desired are those of the West, and thus only available to the extent credit is forthcoming.

The upshot of the arguments of this section is that we cannot expect the existence of the CMEA to serve as a conduit of fluctuations from one member to another (we have purposefully left out discussion of the Soviet Union - whose market power may be able to transmit real effects). As each country tries to balance trade with its partners, there is no mechanism which can spread disequilibrium across borders. If East European economies display a common cyclical variation, it cannot be explained by the fact that these countries trade with each other. *This does not mean that the causes of these cycles must be internal.* Nor does it mean that external shocks cannot be an important part of the explanation. Rather the point of this section has been to argue that the common variation is not a result of the integration of these economies via trade.

Although the STE can insulate itself against autonomous trade flows and the cumulative movements that might follow, there are some external shocks that it cannot avoid. Changes in the terms of trade will affect real income of the STE. How the STE responds depends on the circumstance; the important point is that the insulation of the domestic economy extends only to prevention of second round effects. Changes in the availability of credit can also affect the economy. By allowing the CPE greater capacity to engage in intertemporal substitution, credit affects the time path of output. In particular, in a resource-constrained economy (see Kornai 1979) external credit can reduce the impact of shortages on production. Finally disruptions in the supply of key imported inputs can also have real income effects. This would occur if the inputs could not be produced domestically (in the short run), and if there are limited substitution possibilities in the short run (see Ickes 1984).

Each of these effects can be important. But one should note that each takes the form of an external *shock*. They are not the sort of phenomena that would serve as an endogenous cyclical mechanism. To rely on these sorts of factors to explain the cycles means a different type of explanation than what is common in the literature. It means abandoning the search for an endogenous cyclical mechanism - something that explains the boom, the turning point and the slump - and instead looking to unexpected shocks.

## 3.

There is one aspect of CMEA trade we have neglected so far, Soviet trade behaviour. Given the size of the Soviet Union relative to the other CMEA countries, one might expect the former to transmit a strong influence to the latter. We have already noted that Soviet *cyclical* fluctuations seem unrelated to the CMEA cycles. But what about Soviet trade behaviour? From our argument in section 2 it is clear that the influence of Soviet trade will not be through demand side effects. That is, rising Soviet imports from the CMEA should not be expected to raise output in CMEA countries via (Keynesian) multiplier effects. Rather, we would expect the influence to run in the opposite direction. Soviet exports to the bloc augment domestic production and reduce bottlenecks. Output expands via the operation of the shortage multiplier (Ickes 1984).

The underlying assumption in this analysis is that Soviet exports are exogenous. We suppose that the Soviets determine how much they wish to export to the bloc (presumably based on their desired imports), and that the other CMEA countries are willing to import the quantities made available. This seems to be a plausible assumption for this preliminary stage. Later we shall need to explain more carefully the determinants of fluctuations in Soviet exports.

One way to test the hypothesis that the common variation is caused by Soviet exports is to compare fluctuations in the Soviet export series to the fluctuations in East European Output. Since the mechanism at work here is a bottleneck multiplier, we must look at export quantities rather than values. There is, however, a paucity of data on Soviet exports to the various East European CPE's. Marrese and Vanous (1983) do provide data on Soviet exports to each of the 'Six' in world market prices. These series are broken down into the following categories: machinery and equipment, fuels, non-food raw materials, food and raw materials for food, and industrial consumer goods. We then deflated this series using the unit value indices for market economies (UN Yearbook of Trade Statistics). This should give us a rough idea of the pattern of real trade flows from the Soviet Union to Eastern Europe.

One may ask whether or not Soviet exports to the CMEA fluctuate enough to be responsible for output fluctuations of the East European CPE's. To provide an answer we calculate the coefficient of variation of the growth rates of Soviet exports to each of the CPE's. The results are presented in Table 6.9.

Table 6.9
Variation of real soviet exports to CMEA countries

|  | C.V.* | mean** |
|---|---|---|
| Bulgaria | 91.06 | .13 |
| Czechoslovakia | 149.20 | .05 |
| GDR | 219.86 | .05 |
| Hungary | 126.55 | .09 |
| Poland | 147.61 | .07 |
| Romania | 276.86 | .05 |
| CMEA as a whole | 124.58 | .06 |

$$* \quad CV = \frac{\sigma_g}{\bar{g}} \qquad\qquad g_t = \frac{Y_t}{Y_{t-1}} - 1$$

$$** \quad mean \equiv \bar{g} = \frac{1}{n} \sum_{t=1}^{n} g_t$$

Source: Vienna Institute for Comparative Economic Studies

Comparing these results to those in Table 6.4 (for NMP and Investment) indicates that exports fluctuate more than output or investment. Interestingly, Soviet exports to the bloc as a whole fluctuate more than Soviet output.

The next step is to de-trend the deflated export series. The results are reported in Table 6.10. There are no major surprises. It is interesting to note that the growth rates of exports are higher than that for output (except for Romania). In Table 6.11 we present the correlation between the output residuals and the export residuals (contemporaneously and lagged one period). The correlations are quite weak. Indeed it does not appear that one can identify - via simple correlation analysis - any relationship between these series. One would like to use vector autoregression to search for a more complex relationship, but a paucity of data suggests against it. Thus, while this hardly constitutes a formal test, it does cast doubt on the hypothesis that fluctuations in exports from the Soviet Union 'cause' the East European cycles [17].

## Table 6.10
### Real soviet exports to CMEA countries

| To: | T | $T_2$ | $R^2$ | DW |
|---|---|---|---|---|
| Bulgaria | .158 (11.73) | -.002 (-2.91) | .988 | 1.68 |
| Czechoslovakia | .054 (6.02) | -.001 (-1.40) | .961 | 2.41 |
| GDR | .052 (3.86) | -.0001 (-0.67) | .919 | 1.85 |
| Hungary | .131 (8.52) | -.002 (-3.17) | .971 | 1.32 |
| Poland | .114 (5.48) | -.002 (-1.52) | .946 | 0.70 |
| Romania | .062 (3.91) | -.001 (-1.49) | .873 | 1.87 |
| To 'Six' as a whole | .086 (7.93) | -.001 (-1.95) | .976 | 1.49 |

Source: Vienna Institute for Comparative Economic Studies

## Table 6.11

| | Correlation between NMP residuals and own trade residuals | Correlation between NMP residuals and lagged own trade residuals | Correlation between NMP residuals and overall trade residuals |
|---|---|---|---|
| Bulgaria | .067 | .082 | .366 |
| Czechoslovakia | .058 | .367 | .518 |
| GDR | .256 | -.0001 | .579 |
| Hungary | .374 | .402 | .393 |
| Poland | .193 | .048 | .165 |
| Romania | -.224 | .149 | .526 |

Source: Vienna Institute for Comparative Economic Studies

**4.**

To this point we have identified the cycle in the various CPE's by examining the residuals of the regressions reported in Tables 6.1 and 6.2. The assumption is that there is a secular trend around which output fluctuates. Such a procedure has been standard in macroeconomics for a long time. In effect, one is assuming that the series in question can be decomposed into a secular and a cyclical component. The two effects are decomposed by running a regression of the form:

$$y_t = \beta_0 + \beta_i t + u_t \tag{1}$$

where the $\beta_i$ are parameters, $y_t$ is the natural log of output, and $u_t$ is an error term with mean zero. The time series of the estimated $u_t$'s are then treated as the cyclical component of $y_t$, as in Tables 6.1 and 6.2 above. Notice that the cyclical component is treated as a stationary stochastic process, while the trend is assumed to be deterministic (since the $\cdot i$ are fixed parameters). Such a procedure implies that a unique secular trend can be identified for the period in question. A slowdown in the rate of growth can, of course, be accommodated by employing higher powers of time in equation 1. Nonetheless the secular and cyclical components are treated asymmetrically, since the former is treated deterministically, while the latter is considered to be stochastic.

The rationale for this asymmetry seems to be convention. Why should economic growth be considered to be deterministic? Random shocks, such as changes in the terms of trade or world interest rates, would be expected to alter the equilibrium growth path. Hence an equally plausible hypothesis would be that output follows a random walk with drift. The latter assumption makes the model entirely stochastic, whereas the conventional approach bounds uncertainty by treating the deviations from trend as stationary.

One can attempt to distinguish between the two models using results from Fuller (1976) and Dickey and Fuller (1979). Consider the following regression:

$$y_t = \beta_0 + \beta_1 y_{t-1} + \beta_2 t + \varepsilon_t \tag{2}$$

If the conventional model is correct, and if the residuals follow a first order AR process, we would expect to find $\beta < 1$ in (2). If the correct model is a random walk, however, then we would expect $\beta_1 = 1$. The problem is that conventional tests reject the hypothesis of unit roots too frequently (Fuller 1976, Nelson and Plosser 1982). To circumvent the problem Dickey and Fuller derive a test which involves estimation of:

$$y_t = \beta_0 + \beta_1 y_{t-1} + \beta_2 \Delta y_{t-1} + \beta_3 t + \varepsilon_t \qquad (3)$$

where $\Delta$ is a difference operator. The test centres on whether or not $\beta_1$ = 1. Since conventional tests reject too often, Dickey and Fuller suggest comparing the value of $\tau(\equiv(\beta_1-1)/\sigma_1))$ to the corresponding table in Fuller (1976). The results of such a test are presented in Tables 6.12 and 6.13 (investment).

The results in Tables 6.12 and 6.13 are quite interesting. The estimated values of $\beta_1$ would, on conventional procedures, be deemed unequal to one. Hence we would reject the hypothesis of a unit root. The values of $\tau$, however, suggest a different picture. We fail to reject the hypothesis of a unit root in all cases. Similar results are obtained for investment in the very interesting paper by Mihalyi.

Of course the inability to reject the hypothesis of a unit root does not allow us to conclude that the series are nonstationary. The tests do, however, cast doubt on the conventional procedure. It is thus interesting to inquire as to the implications of nonstationarity for these time series.

Table 6.12

Test for unit roots (NMP)

$$y_t = \beta_0 + \beta_1 y_{t-1} + \beta_2 \Delta y_{t-1} + \beta_3 t + \varepsilon_t$$

| | $\beta_0$ | $\beta_1$ | $\tau(\rho)*$ | $\beta_2$ | $\beta_3$ | $R_2$ | DW | $\rho$ |
|---|---|---|---|---|---|---|---|---|
| Bulgaria | -0.023 (-.199) | 1.074 (11.43) | .801 | 0.14 (0.623) | -.006 (-1.004) | .999 | 2.37 | −.249 |
| Czech | 1.04 (2.39) | 0.795 (8.95) | -2.295 | 0.750 (4.20) | .009 (2.22) | .996 | 1.69 | .066 |
| GDR | 0.87 (1.94) | 0.797 (7.37) | -1.879 | .451 (2.82) | .009 (1.85) | .999 | 2.32 | -.172 |
| Hungary | -.126 (-.199) | 1.040 (7.65) | .244 | -.039 (.143) | -.003 (.544) | .443 | 2.013 | -.008 |
| Poland | 0.918 (2.29) | 0.854 (13.09) | -2.235 | 0.871 (4.75) | .007 (1.85) | .989 | 1.91 | -.074 |
| Romania | 0.733 (1.85) | 0.836 (8.99) | -1.738 | 0.827 (3.63) | .013 (1.66) | .998 | 2.11 | -.203 |
| USSR | −0.119 (-0.32) | 1.043 (13.44) | .554 | -.178 (-0.749) | -.004 (-1.01) | .984 | 1.95 | -.106 |

\* The critical value for n = 25 at .05 level is -3.60 (Fuller 1976)

$y_t \equiv \log (NMP_t)$

# Table 6.13
## Test for unit roots (Investment)
$$i_t = \gamma_0 + \gamma_1 i_{t-1} + \gamma_2 \Delta i_{t-1} + \gamma_3 t + \varepsilon_t$$

|          | $\gamma_0$ | $\gamma_1$ | $\tau(\rho)$* | $\gamma_2$ | $\gamma_3$ | $\overline{R}_2$ | DW | $\rho$ |
|----------|------------|------------|---------------|------------|------------|------------------|------|--------|
| Bulgaria | 0.046      | 0.928      | -0.465        | -.031      | .0006      | .984             | 1.95 | -.106  |
|          | (0.68)     | (6.03)     |               | (-.123)    | (.053)     |                  |      |        |
| Czech    | 0.959      | 0.787      | -1.647        | 0.494      | 0.011      | .981             | 1.94 | -.014  |
|          | (1.707)    | (6.09)     |               | (2.17)     | (.145)     |                  |      |        |
| GDR      | 0.162      | 0.977      | -.267         | 0.472      | -.001      | .992             | 2.11 | -.081  |
|          | (.432)     | (11.40)    |               | (2.130)    | (-0.20)    |                  |      |        |
| Hungary  | 0.282      | 0.963      | -.291         | 0.109      | -.003      | .968             | 2.09 | -.008  |
|          | (0.501)    | (7.58)     |               | (0.45)     | (-.398)    |                  |      |        |
| Poland   | 0.761      | 0.835      | -2.72         | 0.905      | 0.01       | .981             | 1.93 | -.009  |
|          | (2.83)     | (13.74)    |               | (5.52)     | (2.12)     |                  |      |        |
| USSR     | .0005      | 1.08       | .193          | 0.028      | -.003      | .996             | 2.13 | -.117  |
|          | (.001)     | (10.95)    |               | (0.119)    | (-0.528)   |                  |      |        |

\* The critical value for n = 25 at .05 level is -3.60 (Fuller 1976)
$i_t \equiv \log(I_t)$

## 5.

Of what importance is the finding that we are unable to reject the hypothesis of unit roots? There are both empirical and theoretical implications. Let us discuss these in turn.

The implications for the identification of cycles in socialist economies are several. First of all it suggests that we cannot use conventional detrending methods to identify cycles. In order to identify cycles we must use decomposition methods appropriate for stochastic time series (see Beveridge and Nelson 1981). This will allow us to distinguish shocks to the trend from cyclical fluctuations around the trend. It will clearly have important effect on the nature and timing of the cycle. A simple example may be useful. Consider a time series with small fluctuations around trend. Suppose that midway through the sample period a shock occurs that shifts the intercept of the trend. If we estimate a trend for the entire period we will observe smooth fluctuations with strong autoregressive properties (much like the cycles in section 1). If we take into account the shock to the trend, however, we would instead observe the shorter cyclical fluctuations around the two distinct trends. Clearly the observed frequency of the cycle is radically different under the two procedures. And, of course, this problem is magnified when an economy is subject to frequent shocks.

These considerations may help explain the surprising results in section 1. By estimating a model with a deterministic trend, we forced all of the shocks into the cyclical component. This may explain why the resulting cycles possessed such low frequencies. It may be the result of misspecification. Using appropriate decomposition methods we may find an alternative characterisation of cycles in CPE's.

This may alter some of our earlier somewhat negative conclusions. Preliminary work seems to indicate that the *cyclical* components obtained using the Beveridge-Nelson technique show less common variation than the results using the conventional method. The *permanent* components appear more highly correlated. A plausible interpretation would have the common variation be the result of the common (external) shocks. Failure to account for the common shocks in the conventional approach yields low frequency cycles with much common variation. Accounting for these permanent shocks may leave a cycle with less common variation. The investment cycle may reappear as a plausible hypothesis once the shocks to the trend are eliminated.

Nonstationarity has important theoretical implications as well. The deterministic-trend framework is appealing in its simplicity, but inflexible. It is convenient to treat secular phenomena as deterministic, and focus our attention on the cyclical remainder. But by forcing all of the variation onto the cyclical component, we may be magnifying the role of cycles. Moreover, accepting the hypothesis of nonstationarity allows us to drop the asymmetric treatment of trend and cycle.

Once we drop the notion of a deterministic trend it becomes natural to think of cycles in an impulse-propagation framework (Frisch). Economies are subject to periodic shocks. Moreover, shocks tend to persist, due to propagation mechanisms, the identification of which become the focus of our attention. The study of these mechanisms must play an increasingly important role in the analyses of cycles. Why shocks have effects that persist is an important question for macroeconomists studying market and socialist economies. For it is the persistence of disturbances that is the puzzling phenomenon. Students of CPE's have long suggested that planning is conducted 'from the achieved level'. This will clearly lead to a first order autoregressive process if there is a stochastic component to the series. It will be interesting to see the extent to which this simple propagation mechanism will result in time series that look like those we have studied. Eventually, however, we will need to incorporate into our analysis the relationship between output and investment (and determine the direction of causation). Clearly there is a lot to do, evidence that the adoption of the stochastic framework is liberating, suggesting many directions that future research can follow.

Table 6.14
Correlations for 1960-1979

NMP

| | Bulgaria | Czech. | GDR | Hungary | Poland | Romania | USSR |
|---|---|---|---|---|---|---|---|
| Bulgaria | 1.0 | .619 | .838 | .510 | .362 | .167 | .753 |
| Czech. | | 1.0 | .757 | .704 | .394 | .001 | .761 |
| GDR | | | 1.0 | .629 | .601 | .317 | .797 |
| Hungary | | | | 1.0 | .444 | .095 | .446 |
| Poland | | | | | 1.0 | .831 | .385 |
| Romania | | | | | | 1.0 | .090 |
| USSR | | | | | | | 1.0 |

Investment

| | Bulgaria | Czech. | GDR | Hungary | Poland | USSR |
|---|---|---|---|---|---|---|
| Bulgaria | 1.0 | .283 | .416 | .566 | .205 | .438 |
| Czech. | | 1.0 | .737 | .161 | .592 | .773 |
| GDR | | | 1.0 | .545 | .180 | .608 |
| Hungary | | | | 1.0 | -.154 | .421 |
| Poland | | | | | 1.0 | .553 |
| USSR | | | | | | 1.0 |

Correlation between NMP Residuals and Investment residuals

| | |
|---|---|
| Bulgaria | .713 |
| Czechoslovakia | .855 |
| GDR | .758 |
| Hungary | .390 |
| Poland | .936 |
| USSR | .778 |

Source: Vienna Institute for Comparative Economic Studies

125

# Notes

[1] For a review, and critique, of the literature see Ickes 1986. For a recent dissent see Wiles 1982.

[2] See for example the paper by Staller (1964) where various measures of instability - all involving some measure of fluctuations in the growth rate – are presented for a sample of market and planned economies.

[3] One might wonder to what extent the common variation results from the 'Solidarity period'. To assess this, I estimated the equations over the 1960-79 period and calculated the correlation coefficients. The results were quite similar, except for Romania, where there no longer appears to be any correlation with the cycles in Bulgaria, Czechoslovakia, GDR, or Hungary. See Table 6.14.

[4] Compare this to Wiles 1982. Notice that Wiles is not very careful in the means employed to identify the cycles. Of course the fact that there is common variation does not rule out the possibility that there are geo-political explanations, but it reduces the likelihood that politics is the whole story.

[5] For 1973 the percentage of total trade that remained within CMEA was 75% for Bulgaria, 60.5% for Czechoslovakia, 63.4% for East Germany, 60.4% for Hungary, 53% for Poland, 42.4% for Romania, 54% for the Soviet Union. Of course the Soviet Union accounts for the bulk of the intra-CMEA trade for each of the Six. If we exclude the Soviet Union, the numbers are respectively, 21%, 29%, 26.7%, 25%, and 21.4%. See Holzman (1976, p. 71).

[6] See Wiles 1963 and Holzman 1976, 1979 for illuminating discussions of the trade practices of CPE's.

[7] Such studies are difficult to carry out. First one must estimate what a "typical country's" trade behaviour would be, given its GNP and population (etc.). Then one must calculate actual trade volumes, which is made difficult because of trade at intra-CMEA prices (which typically over-state world prices for comparable products, leading to an overstatement of bloc trade). Results of the studies that have been carried out typically show ratios of actual trade to predicted trade to be between 0.50 to 0.75. But as the predicted volume of trade is an estimate, one should report not the ratios, but rather "confidence bands." See Hewett 1980 for a discussion of various studies and the issues involved in their proper interpretation.

[8]  One purpose of the Hungarian reform was to reduce the influence of the FTM. Enterprises in Hungary are thus much freer to trade than their counterparts in the CMEA.

[9]  There is an important exception to this with respect to imported inputs.   This is discussed below in section 4. But even here the multiplier effects are on the supply side.

[10]  Staller's method is to construct a least squares estimate of a country's trade (in current prices) over time, and then divide the standard error of the estimate by the average volume of trade over the period. Staller does this for various pairs of countries, and then aggregates across groupings (OECD, CMEA, LDC's, with US, etc.). He then tests for whether differences in the resulting indices are statistically significant. For the comparisons relevant to us, they are.

[11]  See Ickes 1985 for a discussion of the determination of economic activity in CPE's.

[12]  Nove (1977: 269) notes that: 'If a manager in Omsk cannot freely decide to buy from Minsk, then, evidently he cannot freely decide to buy from Prague or Düsseldorf. Nor can he decide whether the resources of his enterprise should be devoted to supplying the domestic or the foreign market.' But the reverse is also true. In a very real sense the rouble is not convertible *within* the USSR: 'the manager in Omsk cannot turn his money into needed inputs without an allocation certificate issued by *Gosplan* or Gossnab' (276). Since the manager in Omsk cannot freely convert his rubles into goods, how can the man in Prague?!

[13]  Indeed most studies show that the increased flow of trade between CMEA countries is due to trade diversion rather than trade creation. Some of the reasons are explained in the text. For more see Holzman 1979.

[14]  Montias (1980) estimates this discount to be about 35% for Romania's trade in machinery products.

[15]  Indeed the first attempts at such integration collapsed for just such reasons. Khruschev sought to create a division of labour within the CMEA. Romania, a relatively backward country, balked at the prospect of having to specialise in raw materials. Instead Romanian planners went ahead with their own plans to create major steel and petroleum refining industries. For interesting discussions on this issue, see Nove (1970), Marer and Montias (1980), and Holzman (1976).

[16]  Even Portes would accept this statement. His studies of macroeconomic disequilibrium in CPE's have focused on the consumer

goods markets. He accepts the chronic nature of excess demand for intermediate and investment goods. See, for example, Portes and Winter 1980.

[17] Notice that if the correlations in Table 6.10 were high the conclusions that could be drawn would remain weak. For one could alternatively hypothesise that East European demand - caused by economic expansion - led to the growth in exports to the bloc. Examining the correlations does not allow one to discriminate between the two hypotheses. Since there does not appear to be any systematic relationship we avoid this problem.

## References

Bauer, T., (1978), Investment Cycles in Planned Economies, *Acta Œconomica*, Vol. 21, 3.

Beveridge, S. and Nelson, C.R., (1981), A New Approach to Decomposition of Economic Time Series into Permanent and Transitory Components with Particular Attention to Measurement of the 'Business Cycle', *Journal of Monetary Economics*, 7.

Burns, A. and Wesley, M., (1946), *Measuring Business Cycles*, National Bureau of Economic Research.

Dickey, D. A. and Fuller,W.A., (1979), *Distribution of the Estimators for Autoregressive Time Series with a Unit Root*, JASA, 74, 366.

Frisch, Ragnar, (1933), Propagation Problems and Impulse Problems in Dynamic Economics, in *Essays in Honor of Gustav Cassel* , London, Allen and Unwin.

Fuller, W. A., (1976), *Introduction to Statistical Time Series*, New York, Wiley.

Holzman, F. (1976), International Trade Under Communism, Basic Books.

——, (1979), *Some Systemic Factors Contributing to the Convertible Currency Shortages of CPE's*, AER Papers and Proceedings, v. LIX, May.

Ickes, B.W., (1985b), *A Macroeconomic Model for Centrally Planned Economies*, The Pennsylvania State University Working Paper.

——, (1986) *Cyclical Fluctuations in Centrally Planned Economies: A Critique of the Literature*, Soviet Studies, XXXVIII, 1, January.

Klein, P.A. and Moore, G., (1985) *Monitoring Growth Cycles in Market-Oriented Countries*, Cambridge, MA, Ballinger.

Kornai, J., (1979), Resource-Constrained versus Demand-Constrained Systems, *Econometrica*, v. 47.

Marer, P. and Montias, J.M., (eds.) (1980), *East European Trade and Integration*, Bloomington, Indiana University Press.

Marrese, M. and Vanous, J., (1983), *Soviet Subsidization of Trade with Eastern Europe*, Institute for International Studies, Berkeley.

Mihalyi, P., *The Synchronization of Investment Fluctuations in Eastern Europe*.

Montias, J. M., (1980), *Romania's Foreign Trade Between East and West*, in Marer and Montias.

Nelson, C., and Plosser, C., (1982), Trends and Random Walks in Macroeconomic Time Series, *Journal of Monetary Economics*, 9.

Nove, A., (1977), *The Soviet Economic System*, London.

Portes, R., and Winter, D., (1980), Disequilibrium Estimates for Consumption Goods Markets in Centrally Planned Economies, *Review of Economic Studies*.

Pryor, F., (1968), *Discussion*, in Brown and Neuberger.

Rosefielde, Steven, (1974), *Factor Proportions and Economic Rationality in Soviet International Trade ,1955-68*, AER, 64.

Staller, G., (1964), Fluctuations in Economic Activity: Planned and Free-Market Economies, *American Economic Review*, LIV, n. 4.

——, (1967), *Patterns of Stability in Foreign Trade: OECD and Comecon, 1950-63*, AER, LVII, 4.

Tyson, Laura D., (1983), Investment Allocation: A Comparison of the Reform Experiences of Hungary and Yugoslavia, *Journal of Comparative Economics*, 7, 3.

Wiles, Peter D., (1982), *Are There Any Communist Economic Cycles?*, ACES Bulletin, v. 24, no. 2.

# 7 A model of political business cycle in a Soviet-type economy

GUIDO ORTONA

## 1.

Three different approaches can be identified under the general heading of the 'political business cycle problem' with reference to Soviet-type economies (STE'S). Lafay's (1981) approach is the same as for Western countries — the study of movements in or around economic trends due to periodical political occurrences, typically elections. As Ickes (1986) correctly points out, however, in a STE all economic decisions involve a political one, so that in this sense the problem immediately boils down to that of cyclical movements in STE'S *tout court*; a question surrounded, as Dallago (1986) notices, by a remarkable consensus, following Goldmann (1964), Bauer (1978), and others on the same line [1]. In a third sense (the one we will be concerned with in this study), the label applies to the explanation of the periodical occurrence of political reforms, lasting for a while and then, generally abruptly, abandoned. In a way, this problem is the opposite of the traditional one: the point is not to explain how politics influence the economy, but on the contrary how the economy produces changes, which turn out to be cyclical, in political equilibria.

**2.**

The reference model on this subject is due to Nuti and Screpanti (Nuti, 1984 and 1985; Screpanti, 1985). It may be summarised as follows: deeply rooted in the system there is a tendency to overcapitalisation (for reasons explained in the theory of the cycle in STE'S referred to above), and to political centralisation. The two tendencies combine to produce inefficiency. Decentralisation is the only way out, but this unavoidably entails a lessening of political control, which in turn stirs up political unrest. This situation is tolerated up to a point, then repression ensues. The repression cuts the head (hopefully in a figurative sense) of the protest, making room for another phase of decentralisation. It must be stressed that the starting point of the model is the existence of a preference function of the government exogenous with respect to that (or those) of the citizens. Actually, there are only two reasons why the government should embark upon an unpopular overcentralisation line: either the government is trying to implement a specific strategy, for instance of the Olivera (1960) – Wiles (1982) sort, or it is the political system itself that is bound, by its very nature, to resort to such a policy. But in the latter case, too, one could conceivably translate the impacts of the political system into a specific preference function. If we stick to the principle of introducing as few exogenous assumptions as possible, we must, first, reject the hypothesis of an exogenous preference function; and, secondly, postulate a functioning of the political system which is as simple as possible. From this point of view, the situation of the USSR is different from that of other CMEA countries, where the subjection , to different degrees, to a foreign rule may actually require the introduction of an exogenous preference function for the government; and the Nuti-Screpanti model appears to fit quite well with the events of several East-European countries, namely Poland, Hungary and Czechoslovakia. But insofar as at the very root of the respective crises lies the presence of a sort of foreign domination, these situations cannot be considered, even if *normal*, also *typical* of STE'S. Actually, from this point of view the only typical evidence which can be analysed is that of the Soviet Union itself. This evidence may be summarised as follows:

    a) 'Waves' of reforms, with quite a long time span between one another;

    b) within these waves, the reforms proceed in a stop-and-go way;

    c) these waves are usually put to rest quite suddenly, even though the necessity of 'great' reforms is still advocated from many, even high, quarters.

Our problem is that of explaining such evidence without resorting to an *ad hoc* preference function for the government. Consequently, we will try to show that this evidence can be explained if we simply posit the same preference function usually postulated in standard models of political-business cycles in Western countries, i.e. if we posit that the only aim of the government is that of minimising the weighted discontent of the subjects of the economy. As we will see, we must also admit that the government is myopic; this too is an usual assumption in the political-business cycle theory.

## 3.

According to Nuti (1984), in a typical STE 'the problem is not the excessive role of the state... but a quasi-feudal fragmentation and devolution of state power'. Let us borrow this description literally, and let the system be pyramidal. Every tier of the pyramid has sovereign power over a sector of tiers below it, apart from constraints from above, and is held responsible in the perception of the level immediately above for everything that may happen in that sector. The top tier of the pyramid is appointed by the second highest tier according to established procedures (see Gill, 1985). The person in charge of any position may always be removed; we posit that all these persons aim to minimise the probability of losing their post. Label each tier with a letter, with A for the top, and consider an officer in charge of a post on tier, say, G. It is his duty to see that orders flowing from above are executed at best: should this not come about, F risks being fired by E, so F will not forgive G's 'mistakes' (we use for convenience the same symbol for an office and for the corresponding officer). It seems safe to assume that the greater the discontent, the greater the difficulties G will encounter in implementing his orders. So G will do his/her best to keep the discontent to a minimum, given the necessity of fulfilling those orders. Consider now the top tiers of the system. Officers in charge at tier B are under pressure from possible substitutes; they too are interested in minimising the discontent. But the same holds for A: if orders emanating from A are likely to create discontent, this will increase the probability for B-officers to be substituted, so that the latter will try, according to established procedure, to change the A-level officer. So there is a system-wide tendency to avoid discontent. Obviously, this by no means implies a low level of discontent; in addition, the actual policies will depend on the time period over which the discontent has to be minimised. The choice of this period will in turn depend on the institutional features of the system; we will come back to this in §6.


**4.**


We will now leave the political system and turn to the economy. Let us keep on a comparable level of abstraction, and describe it with the following model:

$$Y_t = A_t \ K \ (1 + s)^t \ \pi \ (L_{i,t}^{a_i}) \qquad (1)$$

We use for convenience a Cobb-Douglas production function. The second term is the total product of the (one-commodity) economy. Y is the disposable income; the transforming parameter is encompassed in A. L-terms denote the inputs of labour of *any* workers in the economy, and a-terms the corresponding elasticities, which may be negative or zero; s is a technical progress parameter: we assume for convenience that it is constant. We also assume that the stock of capital is constant.

Let us now suppose that the government implements a *reform*, that is, adopts a policy package bringing about a better use of resources (to be interpreted as a change in A), but involving, in accordance with a given technical relationship, a change in the labour input required of some workers. We express this situation in the simplest way using the following equations:

$$A_t = A_{t-1} \ (1 + F_t) \qquad (2)$$

$$L_{i,t} = L_{i,t-1} \ (1 + r_i \ F_t) \qquad (3)$$

R may be positive, negative or zero. For instance, the decision to substitute a bureaucratic balance sheet control with random quality control will produce an increase in disposable income (due both to saved time and improved quality), while demanding less work from auditing officers, and more from quality controllers.

Next, we postulate that the change in the level of discontent of the ith individual is a function of three arguments, i.e change in disposable income, change in relative income and change in the labour input. We express all this in the equation

$$M_{i,t} - M_{i,t-1} = - m_i \ Ln \ \left( \frac{x_{i,t} \ Y_t}{Y_{t-1}} \right) + g_i \ \left( \frac{L_{i,t}}{L_{i,t-1}} - 1 \right) + \tag{4}$$

$$+ \ h_i \ L_{i,t-1} - u_i \ ln \ (1 + b_i \ F_t)$$

Details are given, for convenience, in footnote [2]. It must be stressed that we assume that wages are independent (in the short and medium term) of labour input.

By definition

$$M_t = \Sigma \ (q_i \ M_{i,t}) \tag{5}$$

where the Qs are factors (constant in the relevant time period) expressing the relative importance of different individuals in the government's perception, presumably depending on the political constitution. We now introduce our two basic hypotheses:

a) the government has no preference function of its own: it simply aims to minimise M;

b) the government has a myopic perception of the effects of its policies.

If we combine the two hypotheses, we can say that the government moves along the reform path according to [3]

$$F_t = - w \ \left( \frac{\delta M_{t-1}}{\delta F_{t-1}} \right) \qquad w > 0 \tag{6}$$

In other words: if at time t-1 the government accelerates the reform, and this produces an increase in the level of discontent, the reform will be given up; if discontent decreases, the reform will be pursued at time t. If at time t-1 the reform is watered down, and this dilution is not welcomed by the people, the reform will be reintroduced at time t; whereas if the diluted form is welcomed there will be a counterreform at time t.

Solving for $F_t$, we then obtain (details of the calculation are given for convenience in footnote) [4]

134

$$F_t = w\Sigma \left[\frac{q_i \, m_i}{(1 + F_{t-1})}\right] + w\Sigma \left[\frac{q_i \, m_i \, \Sigma a_i \, r_i}{(1 + r_i \, F_{t-1})}\right] - \qquad (7)$$

$$- w\Sigma \left[\frac{(-u_i \, b_i \, q_i)}{(1 + b_i \, F_{t-1})}\right] - w\Sigma \, (q_i \, g_i \, r_i)$$

## 5.

In this form, equation 7 includes (in the case of the USSR) possibly a billion parameters, so it is not very useful. A natural step forward involves recognising the existence of social classes or strata, characterised by specific values of the parameters. Research directed at the relevant empirical evidence could be of great interest (see Nuti, 1985). In this preliminary attempt, we simply suppose the existence of three classes:

a) The class of the $N_1$ subjects whose labour input is increased by the reform. r will take the value $r_1 > 0$.

b) The class of the $N_2$ subjects whose labour input is not affected by the reform. r will take the value 0.

c) The class of the $N_3$ subjects whose labour input is reduced by the reform. r will take the value $r_3 < 0$.

Equation 7 may thus be written as

$$F_t = w \left\{ \frac{T}{(1 + F_{t-1})} + \frac{U}{(1 + r_1 \, F_{t-1})} + \frac{X}{(1 + r_3 \, F_{t-1})} - \qquad (8)\right.$$

$$\left. - \Sigma \left[\frac{(-u_i \, b_i \, q_i)}{(1 + b_i \, F_{t-1})}\right] - Z \right\}$$

where

$T = \Sigma \, (q_i \, m_i)$

$U = r_1 \Sigma \, [(q_i \, m_i) \, \Sigma \, (a_i)]$   for the first class

$V = r_3 \Sigma \, [(q_i \, m_i) \, \Sigma \, (a_i)]$   for the third class

135

$$Z = (q_i \, g_i \, r_i)$$

T and U will normally be positive, and X negative. Z will normally be positive [5]. In this situation, we may describe the position of the phase line with the help of the following scheme:

| $F_{t-1}$ | $-\infty$ | $-1-\dfrac{1}{\infty}$ | $-1+\dfrac{1}{\infty}$ | 0 | $+\infty$ | |
|-----------|-----------|-----------|-----------|---|-----------|---|
| $F_t$ | $-wZ$ | $-\infty$ | $+\infty$ | $E = X+T+U-Z+\sum u_i \, b_i \, q_i$ | $-wZ$ | |

The phase diagram will then be of the type illustrated in Fig. 7.1, with the convex part crossing the SW or the NE quadrant depending on the magnitude of the positive and negative terms in eq. 8. It goes without saying that the concave part of the function is meaningless [6].

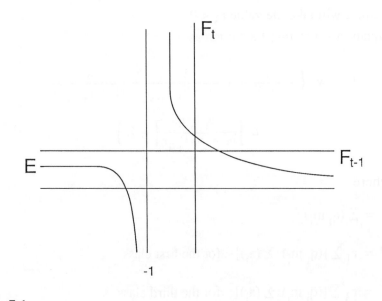

Fig. 7.1

**6.**

If the function passes through the NE quadrant, a reform will take place. This will be the case if there exists a level of reform, even a small one, which can yield a decrease in discontent (see eq. 6). But overall discontent is a weighted sum of the individuals' discontent, and for every level of individual discontent there is a separable function of a (normally positive) labour effect and of two (normally negative) income effects. So discontent will in the aggregate decrease if aggregate income effects more than compensate for the aggregate labour effect. This brings us to an interesting conclusion. It seems safe to argue that labour effects normally precede income effects: after all, one has to work in order to produce goods (or services). The condition that income effects dominate ever since the first period must therefore imply either that the hunger for reforms is so great that people are ready to withstand initially dominating negative labour effects; or that the period (defined as the time during which government cannot change its policy) is long enough to encompass both effects; or both. The two conditions are by no means guaranteed: so it is possible that even in the presence of a general agreement on the necessity of reforms, the government rationally decides not to move in this direction. This may help to explain the traditional inertia of the Soviet leaders towards the adoption of 'obviously necessary' reforms.

As our concern is with reforms, let us in any case take it for granted that our line passes through the NE quadrant, and turn to the next question, i.e.: will the slope of the line at the crossing with the 45° line from the origin be lower than -1 [7] ? This is important because if this is so, F will take in time an explosive path, and if not, a dampened one. We will then have explosive oscillations if in the above mentioned point

$$
w \left\{ \frac{[\sum_n q_i m_i]}{(1 + F_{T-1})^2} + \frac{[r_1^2 (\sum_n q_i m_i) (\sum_n a_i)]}{(1 + r_1 F_{t-1})^2} + \left[ \frac{r_3^2 (\sum_n q_i m_i) (\sum_n a_i)}{(1 + r_3 F_{t-1})^2} \right] - \right.
$$

$$
\left. - \sum_n \left[ \frac{(b_i^2 u_i q_i)}{(1 + b_i F_{t-1})^2} \right] \right\} > 1
$$

(9)

137

In other words, we may expect explosive oscillations if *ceteris paribus*

a) the income effect is large (terms with m);

b) the reaction of the government is strong (factor w);

c) the increase in labour input is large (effect of $r_1$) [8];

d) the elasticity of output with respect to labour is high (terms with a);

e) F in the previous period is low. But *ceteris paribus* this implies high values of g, i.e. of the effect of an increase in work on the level of discontent.

f) Reductions in relative income are large (terms with b) for those strata that are affected by the reform [9].

In short, as seems logical, we can the more easily expect explosive oscillations in the reform policy, the more the three effects (income, relative income and labour) are all simultaneously strong, and the more the government reacts enthusiastically to short-term effects of its policy, i.e. the more the government is weak and/or short-sighted. This is our second conclusion.


## 7.

The case of a phase line passing through the NE quadrant with a slope steeper than 45° is the only one of interest for us. The situation is depicted in Fig. 7.2. Prior to the beginning of our story, the economy lies at the origin of the axes.

At a first sight, one would say the next point should be B. Actually, things are more complicated: the F function is not yet defined, and the effect of reform on discontent is not yet discernible. The government will probably perceive that a reform is welcome, but is not in a position to ascertain the optimal amount of reform. So the first value of F will lie somewhere north of the origin. Three possibilities arise:

a) If the government is very lucky or very wise, the starting value of F will be q. In this case, a continuous reform process will be set in motion [10], defined by a constant value of F.

b) If the government is audacious, with a starting value for F higher than A, the economy will immediately enter into a phase of explosive (presumably not only in the mathematical sense) alternation between reform and counter-reform.

c) If the government starts cautiously with a low level of F, a more or less prolonged period of reform will set in, with alternate stop and go phases, followed by a sudden move to counterreform (and then again, if the government is still alive, to reform, and so on).

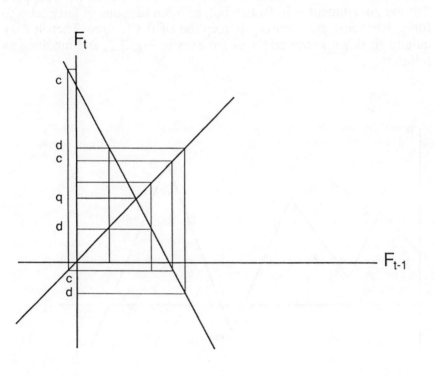

Figure 7.2

If the first level of $F_t$ is q, there will be a constant reform defined by the maintenance of this value of F. If the first level of $F_t$ is for instance the middle value of c, a counterreform will immediately follow. If the first level of F is the middle value of d, there will be another (in this graph) period of reform before the counterreform prevails. The number of reform periods depends on the proximity of the starting value of $F_t$ to q and on the slope of the function, here drawn as a straight line for graphical convenience.

Point c) is our third conclusion: the same path that in the Nuti-Screpanti models is generated by the existence of an exogenous preference function of a strong government may be attributed to the lack of such a function in the behaviour of a weak government.

However, there is also another possibility. According to case c) in the previous section, F changes with time as in Fig. 7.3.

And, as we saw, the more the government is weak and/or myopic, the sooner function F will cross the horizontal axis. Let us now suppose that the government is in fact so but, as often happens in fairy tales to fools, has some extrasensory perception of the future. Then it may quietly sit down at the origin of the axes in Fig. 7.2, and meditate as follows:

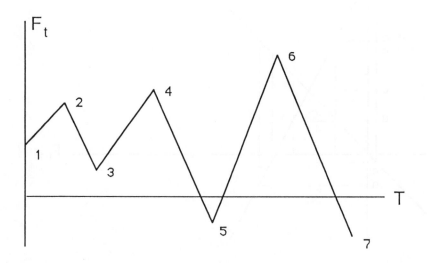

Figure 7.3

'My people want reforms. Well, if I consent I will enjoy for a while a reduction in discontent. This is attractive. But then I will be dragged into a situation where, unless I am able to to leap kangaroo-like from one policy to another, I will have to face a huge discontent. Better not take the risk. After all, people are accustomed to governments which do nothing. The best option is to continue in the traditional way: to recognise that reforms are necessary, but not to implement them'. So a cautious government may decide not to start any reforms, even if the demand for them has been predominant since the first period (see sect. 6).

## 8.

Let us pursue the line of thinking of the last section one step further. If the government does nothing for a sufficiently long time, the demand for reforms may grow to a point where government is forced to implement them. What can then be done to avoid the tragic fate outlined above? Of course, parameters may change. These are independent of the government's actions, with one very important exception: the distributional weights of discontent. These in fact correspond by and large to the audience the different strata of the population enjoy with levels A and B of the power system (see section 3). So a reform-oriented government may try, by appointing the right people and by firing the wrong ones, to reduce the platform of potential opponents to the reform. In other words, we may expect, at the outset of a reform era, a general reshuffling in the political apparatus. For instance, the class of traditional, superfluous bureaucrats *à la Gogol*, even if unaffected in its absolute income and in its labour exertion, may feel threatened with regard to its relative income by a decentralising reform of the type described by Nuti and Screpanti. If it weighs sufficiently heavy in the government's perception of aggregate discontent, this may be sufficient to hinder the reforms, or to rapidly generate unsustainable oscillations. A wise government will therefore try to reduce the political power of this class at the very beginning of a reform phase. There are many indications that in fact something of this kind is happening in the first years of Gorbachev's rule.

## Appendix.  List of symbols

*Note* — in this list the time index is omitted. Symbols introduced for notational simplicity (E, T, U, X, Z) are not included.

A      Constant parameters in the Cobb-Douglas production function referring to the total output of the economy. In addition, A encompasses a factor transforming total output into disposable income. A may be affected by the reform.

$a_i$      Elasticity parameter in the Cobb-Douglas production function referring to a specific participant in the economy.

$b_i$      Parameter linking the share of disposable income accruing to a specific participant in the economy to the implementation of a reform, as expressed by F.

F      Denotes the effect of a *reform*, measured as relative change in the value of A.

$g_i$      Parameter linking the change in discontent of individual $i$ to the relative change in his/her labour input.

$h_i$      Parameter linking the change in discontent of individual $i$ to the absolute level of his/her labour input.

K      Total amount of capital in the economy.

$L_i$      Labour input of individual $i$.

$M_i$      Discontent of individual $i$.

$q_i$      Weight of the discontent of individual $i$ in the perception of the government.

$r_i$      Parameter linking the relative change in labour input of individual $i$ to the implementation of a reform, measured by F.

s      Technical progress parameter in the production function of the economy.

$u_i$      Parameter linking the discontent of individual $i$ to his/her share in total disposable income.

$V_i$      Share of disposable income accruing to individual $i$.

$v_i$      Ratio of $V_i$ to Y, the total disposable income.

w      Parameter linking the change in reform policy (measured by F) to the change in aggregate discontent, due in turn to a change in reform policy in the previous period.

$x_i$      Equals $\dfrac{v_{i,\,t}}{v_{i,\,t-1}}$ (see above).

Y      Total disposable income.

## Notes

[1] For the very existence of cyclical movements in NMP's growth rate in STE's, see Ickes (1986).

[2] *Labour effect*: It seems sensible to assume that discontent is a function both of the relative increase in labour input (a 10% in-

142

crease is worse than a 5%) and of the starting level (a 10% increase if one works 2 hours a day is better than a 10% increase if one works 8 hours a day). The function has the simplest possible form consistent with these assumptions. h will be zero if the labour input is unchanged.

*Absolute income effect*: Let $v_{i,t} Y_t$ be the disposable income of the i-th individual at time t, and the utility function of income be

$$-M_{i,t} = m_i \, \text{Ln} \, (v_{i,t} \, Y_t)$$

Then

$$-M_{i,t} -(-M_{i,t-1}) = m_i \, \text{Ln} \, (v_{i,t} \, Y_t) - m \, \text{Ln} \, (v_{i,t-1} \, Y_{t-1}) =$$

$$= m_i \, \text{Ln} \, \left[ \frac{(v_{i,t} \, Y_t)}{(v_{i,t-1} \, Y_{t-1})} \right]$$

If we call $x_{i,t}$ the ratio of the two values of v and multiply throughout by $-1$, we obtain the expression in the text.

*Relative income effect*: We suppose the share $V_i$ of disposable income accruing to individual i to change i according to the following rule:

$$V_{i,t} = V_{i,t-1} \, (1 + b_i \, F_t)$$

Where b may be negative, zero, or positive. We also suppose that

$$-M_{i,t} = u_i \, \text{Ln} V_{i,t}$$

Then

$$M_{i,t} - M_{i,t-1} = - u_i \, \text{Ln} V_{i,t} + u_i \, \text{Ln} V_{i,t-1} = - u_i \, \text{Ln} \, (1 + b_i \, F_t)$$

[3] It may be of interest to note that if we add to this function an additional argument independent of M we get a (not yet explored) new class of models, where the government has an exogenous preference function constrained by the need to hold down the discontent.

[4] From eq.3,

$$\frac{L_{i,t}}{L_{i,t-1}} = 1 + r_i \, F_i$$

143

and from eqs 1, 2, and 3,

$$\frac{Y_t}{Y_{t-1}} = (1 + F_t)\ (1 + s)\ \pi\ (1 + r_i\ F_t)^{a_i}$$

Eq. 4 then becomes:

$$M_{i,t} - M_{i,t-1} = - m_i\ Ln\ \{x_{i,t}\ [(1 + F_t)\ (1 + s)\ \pi\ (1 + r_i\ F_t)^{a_i}\ ]\} +$$

$$- u_i\ Ln\ (1 + b_i\ F_t) + h_i L_{i,t-1} \qquad \text{(4 bis)}$$

Then, using eq. 5, we get for eq. 6

$$F = \frac{- w\delta\Sigma\ (q_i\ M_{i,t-1})}{\delta F_{t-1}} = - w\Sigma\ \left(\frac{q_i\ \delta M_{i,t-1}}{\delta F_{t-1}}\right) \qquad \text{(6 bis)}$$

From eq. 4 bis, the typical derivative entering this sum will be, considering time t for notational simplicity:

$$\frac{\delta M_{j,t}}{\delta F_t} = \frac{- m_j}{(1 + F_t)} - m_j\ \Sigma\ \left[\frac{a_i\ r_i}{(1 + r_i\ F_t)}\right] \frac{- u_j\ b_j}{(1 + b_j\ F_t) + g_j\ r_j}$$

Hence by aggregation eq.7 obtains.

[5] The full expression for Z is $-w\Sigma\ q_i\ g_i\ r_i$. Q is a weighting factor; g is the derivative of the discontent with respect to relative change in labour; r determines the change in labour requirement as a consequence of the reform policy. Hence:

$q > 0;$
$g > 0,$

except for the marginal cases of people desiring to work more-cases that we may safely assume to be offset by in the aggregation;

$$r > 0,\ 0\ or < 0$$

according to the direction of the change in labour. Hence Z may be considered the sum of a positive and of a negative term. U is positive, except in the absurd case that the overall elasticity of output with respect to labour is negative. X will be negative, except for the same situation. It may easily be shown that if Z is negative, the economy will be characterised by a continuous reform, an uninteresting situation for our purposes.

[6] Since in that area $F<-1$, and $Y<0$.

[7] The slope of the function may bypass $-1$ in the first quadrant. But as far as the oscillations of F are concerned, this case is equivalent to one of the two 'pure' cases of F lower or greater than $-1$, depending on where the change occurs with respect to the $45^\wedge$ line.

[8] This may be checked by taking the derivative of the term with $r_1$ in eq.9. This derivative will always be $>0$ for $r_1$ and $F_{t-1} >0$.

[9] The proof is the same as for the effect of $r_1$. See fn. 8.

[10] Clearly, however, this would imply changes in the parameters; a process that in a more sophisticated model of this family could better be supposed to be continuous.

# References

Bauer, T. (1978), 'Investment Cycles in Planned Economies', *Acta Oeconomica*, 3, 1978.

Dallago, B. (1986), 'Interpretation of Fluctuations and Cycles in Soviet-Type Economies', paper presented to the meeting on *Regulation, cycles et crises dans les économies socialistes*, Paris, march.

Gill, G. (1985), 'Institutionalisation and Revolution: Rules and the Soviet Political System', *Soviet Studies*, 2.

Goldmann, J. (1964), 'Fluctuations and Trends in the Rate of economic Growth in Some Socialist Countries', *Economics of Planning*, 2.

Ickes, B. (1986), 'Cyclical Fluctuations in Centrally Planned Economies: a Critique of the Literature', *Soviet Studies*, 1.

Lafay, J.D. (1981), 'Empirical Analysis of Politico-Economic Interactions in East European Countries', *Soviet Studies*, 3.

Nove, A. (1969), 'Cyclical Fluctuations under Socialism', in M. Bronfenbrenner (ed.), *Is the Business Cycle Obsolete?*, Wiley & Sons, New York.

Nuti, D.M. (1984), 'Economic Crisis in Eastern Europe: Prospects and Repercussions', EUI Working Papers 26, Florence.

Nuti, D.M. (1985), 'Political and Economic Fluctuations in the Social-
   ist System', EUI Working Paper 156, Florence.
Olivera, J. (1960), 'Cyclical economic Growth under Collectivism',
   *Kyklos*, 2.
Screpanti, E. (1985), 'A Model of the Political-Economic Cycle in
   Centrally Planned Economies', paper presented to the second
   meeting of the AISSEC, Trento, Italy.
Wiles, P. (1982), 'Are there any Communist Cycles?', *ACES Bulletin*,
   2.

# 8 Changes in the socialist economic system

JANUSZ BEKSIAK

The roots of fluctuations and economic crises in socialist countries are in the character and dynamics of their traditional socio-economic system. It is necessary, therefore, to analyse the long-term changes in this system.

We call 'traditional' a system adopted by all socialist countries for long periods of time. Based on a long-lasting tradition and tested in very different situations, this method of control is highly persistent in spite of the generally held opinion that it leads to a low level of economic efficiency. The traditional system is characterised by the primacy of politics over economics, by the existence of centralised, hierarchic administration and by the preference for mainly command management instruments.

This system in its first version emerged after some small adaptations from the war-time variant of the Soviet economic system. In Poland (and in many other East-European countries) this system was introduced and consolidated in the late forties and the early fifties. This first version (stage) I call the Traditional System I or Command Economy System.

In this system, the organisational structure of the central authorities was vertically expanded and formed a multi-level system, while horizontal segmentation was relatively less developed. When compared with all other variants of the control system applied in the post-war period so far, this early system reveals the highest degree of concentration of economic power.

The central economic plan is used as the main instrument of management. It consists of a set of commands addressed to economic organisations. These commands are supported and reinforced by means of rewards and penalties, mainly by increasing or decreasing the workers' incomes. Apart from retail prices of consumer goods, prices are not used as operative instruments of control.

In this system, the use of the term 'enterprise' to denote an economic organisation is hardly justified. These organisations have formally a legal status, separate resources and executive organisation. But their resources are at the free disposal of their superiors and their managers have to be obedient members of central administration. This is why I call them 'ostensible enterprises' [1].

In the sphere of relations between enterprises, the system discussed almost totally excludes market relations. Even when applying formal rules of trade contracts, the central authorities transform them into another form of hidden central distribution. Market relations exist only between socialist enterprises on the one hand, and households or private enterprises, on the other. Even this narrow and disintegrated market is limited by current policies of the central authorities. Money as a 'liquid good' is totally, or almost totally excluded from the activity of socialist enterprises and from their mutual contacts. Some fraction of currency becomes a liquid good only when it comes into the hands of workers and private enterprises.

Tasks given to enterprises are mainly formulated in terms of gross output, which makes the system highly expansive, and encourages enterprises to expand their activity with almost unlimited demand for factors of production. This creates a permanent shortage of many (if not most) factors of production and final goods [2].

Summing up, the system is rather simple and consistent. The instruments used by central authorities are mostly homogeneous. There is also a correspondence between instruments and organisational structures. Due to these advantages the central authorities are able to concentrate national resources in order to implement bold and ambitious undertakings. There is however, a danger of easily undertaking unrealistic tasks which may adversely affect future economic growth and socio-economic evolution. In practice this takes the form of the so-called 'forced' growth programs which consist of: a high and increasing amount of investment, which is scattered through many industries;

the introduction of capital-intensive technology, based on wasteful exploitation of human and natural resources.

In the described system there are significant internal contradictions. I think that four of them are of particular importance.

First, the control system based chiefly on commands is inevitably bound to disregard the reasonable limits of their applicability. In an attempt to make their control as selective as possible, the central authorities tend to issue so many commands at the same time, that, in spite of an high concentration of economic power, contradictory orders are issued and the responsiveness of the central authorities to these contradictions becomes slower (since the capacity of the information system is limited).

Secondly, the sluggishness of the system is due not only to the fact that central authorities are unable to perform their excessive duties successfully. The system has an in-built tendency to hamper the initiative of managers and workers in the enterprises. As a result we have, on the one hand, bold and energetic actions of the central authorities, and, on the order, slow reactions of economic administration and enterprises whose own interests prompt them to implement planned tasks with least effort, to disinform the superiors, and to avoid innovations.

Thirdly, there is an in-built contradiction between rigid, concentrated and directively guided production and distribution, and a considerable freedom of choice of individual consumption, profession and job. The consumer goods market and the labor market exist side by side with the production apparatus in which market mechanisms are missing. This causes permanent discrepancies between supply and demand. Combined with expansive tendencies in enterprises, it cannot but generate a permanent disequilibrium. In turn, the market shortage adversely affects the quality of labor.

Fourthly, this system does not promote social integration and does not encourage people implementing directive plans to accept common goals as their own. On the contrary: it tends to generate indifference and submissiveness combined with frustration and dissatisfaction with the low effects of great efforts and sacrifices.

Such a system acts in two opposite directions: it simultaneously stimulates and hampers the economic activity of the people. It stimulates mainly the expansion of investment. The strong drive to invest is characteristic both for the central authorities and for managers. At the same time this system creates numerous obstacles not only for innovations but for any individual entrepreneurship. It means a wasteful use of a serious part of the economic potential and social energy.

The negative features of the Traditional System I, new problems and economic difficulties, experience gained by managers, and social pressures — all these things led to transformations in the traditional system. These transformations took place in Poland in the late fifties and the early sixties. With the passage of time numerous, but slight changes were introduced into the system. A series of small, partial 'reforms' and some spontaneous processes during the two decades brought about only a small number of new elements, but significantly rearranged the whole traditional control system. Similar tendencies appeared in the majority of socialist countries. As a result, the second variant (phase) of the traditional system emerged. This Traditional System II is a relaxed command economy.

There are significant differences in the organisational structure of the central authorities. In comparison with Traditional System I, these organs are more segmented. This is partly a result of the spontaneous expansion of the economic bureaucracy. Moreover, under the pressure of managers the lower and local units of the hierarchy are gaining a greater degree of power. This complicated segmentation of the control apparatus is only partly justified by the needs of the division of labor. To a large extent it consists of the deconcentration of economic power, which sometimes takes the dangerous form of multi-headed structures.

Such changes are often made under the watchword of decentralisation of management. But this decentralisation has a peculiar character. First, it affects mainly the bureaucratic hierarchy and gives less freedom to enterprises. The result is that the flexibility of the system improves slightly, while the detrimental consequences of the deconcentration of power become even more evident. Enterprises are still guided mainly by means of commands but they are subordinated to a greater number of superior organs. Thus, in this system the possibility of contradictions between directives is even greater that in the previous one. At the same time this fact gives some unexpected freedom to enterprises. Secondly, in practice power transferred to a lower level can easily be taken back whenever its recipient refuses to act according to the expectations of its superiors. In this situation economic organisations become 'until further orders' enterprises. The whole organisational system is not only complicated but also unstable. Its individual elements operate under great uncertainty, and are trained to anticipate the intentions of superior organs.

In this system, as in the previous one, a central plan consists of orders to be executed by enterprises. These orders, however, are more general, less numerous, and are not as strictly enforced. While sticking to commands as their main instruments of management, the central authorities are more inclined to make greater use of what we can call 'non-directive, non-price-type (N,N)' tools. We may distinguish two main categories of N,N's: pure and 'hybrids'. Pure N,N's are non-price expressions and evaluations of economic activities preferred by superiors, amplified by bonuses paid for introducing new products, for selling additional amount of goods, etc. In the more sophisticated variant these rewards are not directly attached to individual events but to 'bunches' of events united by various indicators and coefficients. 'Hybrids', in turn, are a mixture of orders, price-type magnitudes and pure N,N's. Examples: obligatory, predetermined amounts of profits; the so-called 'normative costs'; separate, centrally assigned money funds.

In this system prices are more active than in the Traditional System I. This results from the fact that greater importance is attached to amounts expressed in value terms (profitability, costs, money funds, etc.). Prices do exert some impact on the behavior of enterprises. In most cases, however, this impact is not controlled by the central authorities. This is so, because prices are not used as operative management instruments; in most cases they are mechanically based on costs of production.

The central distribution of resources is still the basic form of goods circulation between economic organisations, although the system allows some (rather narrow) freedom of choice of contractors and terms of deliveries. Such 'horizontal links' appear mainly as exceptions or as an informal relaxation of rigid regulations. In this way at the local level there appear quite provisional and disconnected elements of market relations. Given their rather informal character and the monopolistic position enjoyed by many actors these enclaves of market are poorly submitted to the control of the central authorities. The positive aspect of this situation is that these contacts make the whole economic system more flexible than was the case in the Traditional System I.

The transition from the first to the second stage has not changed the fundamental features of the traditional system: its rigid, hierarchic structure, and the prevailing role played by commands and central distribution. What is particularly important: the preference for the forced growth programs has remained unchanged. Consequently, the main deficiencies of the system remain.

The second version of the system introduces some new elements which ease some limitations and diminish contradictions but, at the same time, themselves generate new contradictions.

First, formally, the autonomy of enterprises is insignificant. In practice, however, their position is now stronger because they retain their monopolistic status and also because of the contradictions between the various instruments of management applied by multi-headed structures. Central control over the economy has been weakened, but without bringing advantages which could be expected if enterprises were free to act on their own and to have direct mutual contacts.

Secondly, mixed ('hybrid') instruments are a highly imperfect substitute for market-type control. They encourage enterprises to bargain for easier directive tasks and to minimise efforts needed to fulfil these tasks. Numerous specified funds and limitations are narrowing the scope of manoeuvre of enterprises, they encourage a wasteful use of resources in some fields and excessive economising in others, and do not allow enterprises to carry out their activity in a continuous manner. As a consequence enterprises tend to avoid innovations, as well as long-term undertakings.

Thirdly, the use of gross output as main indicator of the enterprises' performance, coupled with greater freedom of action gained by enterprises, add up to strengthen the expansive tendencies of enterprises, and creates permanent disequilibrium in the production sphere and in the consumer goods market (the 'sellers' market' or open inflation).

Fourthly, the system of management as a whole is highly complicated and disintegrated. The activity of individual enterprises and of the whole economy is divided into many incompatible fragments (branch and territorial divisions, funds and limits, various calculating methods, etc.). This splits the economic relationships and leads to the situation when the solution of one dilemma is bound to create new dilemmas. The above described 'sectional' management prevents managers from viewing their problems from a wider perspective and favours narrow-mindedness. Particular economic events are often shaped by a number of parallel influences acting at the same time. Directives as well as other control information come from many different sources and are formulated in various forms — of orders, prices, indicators, etc. — even though they refer to the same problems. This leads to inevitable contradictions in the process of management. Such a control system is a source of uncertainty, both to enterprises and central authorities. While retaining its centralised and directive character, the system becomes unable to guide the national economy efficiently.

In the course of analysing the traditional economic system we described some of the mechanisms and contradictions of the economic life. In general, they consist in the contradictory impact of the control system which at once strongly stimulates and hampers economic activity and its development. On the one hand, such a system favours ambitious, forced growth programs and gives difficult planned tasks to economic organisations. On the other hand, it deprives these organisations and individuals of freedom of economic activity, discourages them to undertake innovations, grants poor remuneration for entrepreneurship and initiative.

On the base of this analysis we may make some final conclusions. First, that above described way of achieving economic growth performed within the framework of the traditional control system creates mechanisms which automatically reproduce and strengthen the above mentioned tendencies and contradictions. Secondly, the total of the afore-discussed contradictory processes must lead to economic breakdowns and social conflicts. No economy can function in this way and no society can stand it for a longer time without serious disturbances. Thirdly, the long-term evolution of the traditional system and a prolonged domination of forced growth strengthen all these contradictions, which means that with the passage of time we may expect deeper economic crises coupled with social and political ones.

These negative phenomena may be avoided or at least softened by means of general and thorough reforms.

There are two basic types of economic reforms in socialist countries: first, a 'managerial' reform, conducted by the central authorities and aimed at satisfying the aspirations of managers; second, introducing essential changes into the whole socio-economic structure. The second kind of reform has never been practically completed.

What are the main features of the managerial reforms undertaken many times in various socialist countries?

First, the central authorities remain as a center, guiding the whole economy but mainly by means of non-directive instruments. Their plans are not formulated in terms of directives to be implemented. Both central plans as well as plans of individual enterprises are plans 'for themselves'. The central authorities have to apply market-type instruments to guide the behavior of enterprises and households, and to conduct a monetary policy. In order to function effectively the system needs the 'money brake' policy (also called the 'hard budget constraints' policy), i.e. the policy of preventing excessive financing of enterprises and consumers which would lead to disequilibrium and economic disorder.

Such a change in the status and function of the central authorities calls for a drastic reduction of the bureaucratic apparatus so characteristic of the traditional system (elimination of branch ministries, trusts, unions of enterprises, central organs of cooperatives, etc.). Such a reduction, however, to some extent goes beyond the scope of managerial reform.

Secondly, enterprises are free — with few and rather stable con-straints — to carry out their business, i.e. to decide what, how, and for whom to produce. They act on the principle of 'self-financing'. With some limitations they resemble private enterprises (business organisa-tions) even though they are owned by the state.

Thirdly, relations between economic units are of market character and prices (including wages, interests, rents, etc.) are the main instru-ments by means of which the central organs influence the market and enterprises influence each other. In drafting such reforms it is usually stipulated that some prices should be fixed by the central authorities, and all others by the market mechanism. The system may work efficiently under the condition that prices have a parametric character, which means that they are not determined by individual enterprises. This can be ensured by competition and elimination of monopolies. As this concerns the position of main economic actors, this aspect of the reform goes at least partly beyond the scope of the managerial reform.

Fourthly, self-management. The features pointed out so far have been mostly the same for both types of the economic reform. But widespread introduction of self-management institutions at all levels of economic life is specific to the second type of the reform. For it means that the central authorities are to be controlled by the society, and that managers of individual enterprises are controlled by the workers. These facts would essentially change the whole socio-economic system.

Analysis of the two Polish reforms initiated in 1972 and in 1982 re-veals that most of the afore described transformations were made only partially, half-heartedly, and were highly inconsistent. There were negligible changes in the structure and activity of the central authori-ties. Numerous intermediate organs of the bureaucratic apparatus continue to exist. Central and local administration, which was never reformed, very quickly returned to old practices of command man-agement. The workers' self-management is subjected to strong pres-sures. In this situation the reformed enterprise becomes closer and closer to the above described 'until further orders' enterprise.

To sum up: there is a state of permanent conflict between reform ac-tivity and the deeply-rooted traditional methods of exercising control over economic life. This leads us to the conclusion that the Managerial Reformed System is rather unstable and reveals a tendency to return to the traditional system. The experience of many other socialist coun-tries seems to support this opinion.

All the above described processes of system transformation can be classified into three main groups.

First: frequent, small, partial 'improvements' (reorganisations, local administrative reforms, price and wage 'regulations' etc.). Such changes usually occur under the pressure of current needs and difficulties. They are introduced in order to rationalise some fragments of the system or — in many cases — as a justification for doing nothing. As a consequence, most of them have a superficial character. I call them 'kaleidoscopic' changes because they give permanent rearrangements of the same elements [3]. They, nevertheless, change the whole system, but instead of improving it they rather increase its instability.

Secondly: general and much more essential reforms of the system introduced by the central authorities. They are either made under the pressure and with the active participation of the masses or they are made only by managers and for managers. Even if they are not successful, these reforms give rise to significant changes in the system. But historical experience shows that the results of these reforms are in practice different from the initially designed lines of transformation. This 'drift' results from the action of the next category of dynamic processes.

Thirdly: spontaneous evolution of the socio-economic structures; changes in the behavior of actors who fight for more freedom and power, for a better life and better position in the structure, etc. Such activity gradually changes the whole system. As an example, we can mention two such long-term processes: a) changes in the relation between the national top management and other parts of the administration, which leads to a deconcentration of economic power, b) the development of patron-client relations, substituting the formal vertical relations by informal ones. Changes of this kind are responsible for the spontaneous transformation of the Traditional System I into Traditional System II and for the tendency of the Reformed System to come back to the Traditional System.

As a conclusion, let us make an attempt to outline a general scheme of changes in the economic system and the main directions of its dynamics, assuming that the main features of this system remain unchanged. Here we assume that the second type of reform (i.e. the reform changing not only the control methods but also, and in the first place, the socio-economic structure of the system) has not been implemented.

We start with the Traditional System I which characterised the original socialist economic system (figure 8.1). If the functioning of this system does not lead directly to its break-down ( which the experience of some countries shows to be possible ), as a rule, it switches to the

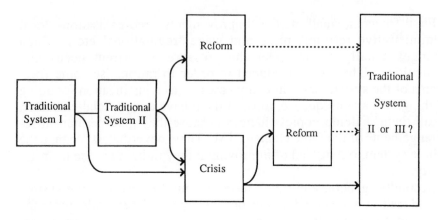

Figure 8.1

Traditional System II. It is a result of the self-activating evolution of the traditional system.

The Traditional System II may, in turn, be reformed, or it leads to crisis.

In the first case, if this reform does not eliminate all the fundamental features of the old system (which means that it is to be a managerial reform) the new system will tend to revert to Traditional System II. As we know from the history of the socialist countries, the maintenance of the reform calls for recurrent reforming activity to counteract the drifting of the system from the direction designed by the reform.

In the second case, there are no grounds to expect that this situation will change spontaneously, i.e. that the crisis will come to an end by itself. Such a crisis does not activate any automatic mechanisms of selection capable of eliminating weaker economic units and supporting more efficient and dynamic participants of economic life. In this situation we can expect alternatively: a) a slow movement in the direction of normalisation along the lines of the Traditional System, b) an introduction of the managerial reform.

As the initial situation is extremely inconvenient, the last solution seems to be the most difficult and the least probable. It is easy, however, to see that in all these alternative situations the system will tend to drift towards some traditional variant.

Finally, we come to the conclusion that all the afore-analysed alternative lines of change lead to the Traditional System II or some newer version of the Traditional System (Traditional System III?). After that

— without removing the fundamental features of the system — we may expect the repetition of one of the afore-described series of changes.

## Notes

[1]   Cf: J. Beksiak, 'Enterprises and Reform; the Polish Experience', *European Economic Review* , vol.31, 1-2, 1987.
[2]   It is easy to see that my opinion on the causes of this shortage differs from that of Professor Janos Kornai (*Economics of Shortage*, 1980).
[3]   I think that this category is close (maybe almost identical) to the Tamas Bauer 'perfectioning' of the system (cf.: T. Bauer, Reforming or Perfectioning the Economic Mechanism in Eastern Europe, European University Institute, Florence, Working Paper No. 86/247).